California Medical Marijuana Dispensary and Grower's Guidebook

A comprehensive guide for creating a medical marijuana dispensary, collectively growing medical marijuana, and operating in the current legal environment.

Table of Contents

California Medical Marijuana Dispensary and Growers' Guidebook: Everything you need to know about opening a marijuana dispensary and/or legally growing medical marijuana.

Authors:

Charles Restivo is an entrepreneur with a background in finance and accounting, including employment at top accounting firms in Santa Barbara, CA. Early in his career, he spent a number of years auditing 501(c)(3) non-profit corporations and became familiar with internal operations. In his position at West End Partners, a local boutique investment firm that evaluated and partnered with failing businesses in order to restructure them, Mr. Restivo gained extensive knowledge of business valuation, acquisitions and consulting. He is a UCSB graduate with an Honors degree in Economics.

Mr. Restivo has been a long-time medical marijuana advocate and has worked with a number of collectives over the last six-plus years. Locally, he was an active demonstrator and dedicated participant in the promotion of Proposition 19, the 2011 California initiative to legalize the use of marijuana.

Mr. Restivo was instrumental in obtaining Santa Barbara's first medical marijuana dispensary permit. Through this process, he gained a wealth of knowledge in the ever-evolving and somewhat controversial topic of medical marijuana dispensaries, including what is required to establish and run a successful storefront dispensary.

Through his own experience in establishing and running a collective, Mr. Restivo has had interactions with local police, district attorneys and federal DEA officers. Fortunately, these confrontations ended in only one minor possession violation. However, these interactions were an integral part of his learning process. Mr. Restivo has heard first-hand what the other side, the prosecuting district attorneys, consider "legal" and what specific details they are currently focusing on to pursue legal action. His numerous hours in court sessions and attorney briefings provide him with a unique, even priceless perspective on the medical marijuana laws.

Mr. Restivo has devoted himself to attendance medical marijuana conferences, relevant city council meetings and has extensively researched California's medical marijuana laws over the last five years.

Currently, Mr. Restivo continues to consult with private businesses, including dispensaries, retail boutiques, salons, and entertainment companies.

William Britt has over thirteen years' experience working with attorneys and has attended over 500 court proceedings throughout Southern California, reading numerous police reports, listening to testimony from experts, police and witnesses, reviewing cannabis evidence, providing reports with weights, photos, estimates of plant yields, etc., and testifying on issues such as cultivation crop yields, methods of distribution, and patterns of use by medical and non-medical users.

He has investigated more than 300 individual cases and testified as an expert on cannabis over 80 times. He has heard police officers testify in court at least 200 times, and examined, evaluated, weighed and photographed cannabis plant material at least 60 times.

From January 2007 to the present, he has worked as amicus curae to several state and federal courts and jurists, including courts in the counties of Los Angeles, Orange, Riverside, San Bernardino, San Diego and Ventura.

He has spent over 1,000 hours interviewing defendants and witnesses, qualified medical cannabis patients, recreational users of cannabis, doctors and police officers, including discussions on legal aspects, patterns of personal use and cultivation techniques. He has also visited and inspected numerous indoor and outdoor legal medical cannabis cultivation sites.

Mr. Britt is a court-qualified expert witness on all issues regarding marijuana, including:

- Appraisal of cannabis value on both a wholesale and retail basis
- Patterns of use of cannabis by qualified patients and methods of ingestion
- Cannabis yields and different formulas used by law enforcement
- Cannabis cultivation methods, both indoor and outdoor
- California Proposition 215 and the Medical Marijuana Program Act (SB 420)
- Methods of acquiring marijuana, such as collectives, co-ops, and the black market

In July 2004 he worked with and advised Long Beach Police Chief Anthony Batts to create police guidelines for officers who encounter qualified medical cannabis patients who use, possess, or transport marijuana in the city of Long Beach.

Mr. Britt has educated doctors on guidelines for recommending cannabis, patterns and methods of use by patients, and effects and benefits of use for patients with chronic pain. He has taught continuing education at UC Irvine Medical School of Pain Management and has been a guest speaker at USC's Keck School of Medicine regarding clinical applications of cannabis.

Over the last fourteen years, Mr. Britt has spoken at numerous community and healthcare provider meetings in southern California, working to educate healthcare professionals, law enforcement officials and politicians on Proposition 215, SB 420 and the benefits of medicinal cannabis.

Mr. Britt has over eight years of prior accounting experience. He also founded (in 1998) and currently manages the Association of Patient Advocates (APA), a nonprofit organization that assists disabled and chronically ill patients to gain access to healthcare information and social services. The APA works with healthcare providers to advocate for patient rights, to improve services and to include the patient in healthcare policy decisions.

Introduction:

The goal of this manual is to provide readers with the tools they need to get started in today's rapidly changing medical marijuana industry. We specifically focus on how to open and operate a California medical marijuana collective, as well as how to legally grow medical marijuana within the state of California. If you have ever started another business in the past, you may find some of this information redundant; however, we didn't want to leave any information uncovered. This book was published in August 2012 and offers the most current information available.

In this book, we delve deeply into dispensary operations, from current state laws to day-to-day operations, as well as how to comply with the various state agencies. Our approach is to provide you with as many resources as we can in order for you to successfully open and operate a medical marijuana dispensary, delivery service and/or grow operation under the guidelines set forth by the state of California.

We strongly suggest that you read the book from beginning to end before you make any business decisions, and that you take notes and flag areas to re-read as questions arise. However, if you need a quick answer, refer to the table of contents for a specific topic. As you may know, the California medical marijuana industry is still evolving, and your search for knowledge should not stop with this or any other book. Please visit our website or email us if you have any questions. We also encourage you to submit feedback. Thank you for purchasing this book, and we hope you are pleased with the information we have provided.

As a starting point, medical marijuana (and its usage) needs to be treated much differently than recreational marijuana (which is *illegal* in California). There are very specific guidelines that need to be followed to ensure that any marijuana activities you take part in are classified as being for medical purposes only. Please note that, although dispensaries require business-like qualities to survive, these are **not-for-profit entities** that are very complex and are fundamental for operating in this industry.

People become involved in the medical marijuana business for a number of reasons. Over the past 15 years, since medical marijuana has become legal, thousands of people have gotten involved in this industry, for various reasons. Some are marijuana activists who strongly believe in the medicinal use of the product, others are people who use medical marijuana and want better, safer access to it, and still others simply enjoy the uplifting effects of marijuana. Many people are attracted to the business side, the opportunity to be self-employed, the flexible hours, and the excitement of being in the forefront of an emerging industry that has billion-dollar yearly potential. Please note that, while some people are attracted to the potential for financial gain, your written plans must comply with the **not-for-profit** objective. Accordingly, if you are interested in this industry only for financial gain, you should be aware that for-profit marijuana entities are illegal, and you should probably consider a different business venture.

With that being said, here is a summary of what you will need to do to get started in the California medical marijuana industry:

1. Get a doctor's recommendation to use and grow medical marijuana
2. Decide what medical marijuana profession you wish to become involved in:
   a. Start a collective to help distribute medicinal marijuana to qualified patients, or
   b. Grow medical marijuana, or
   c. Both.
3. Get organized:
   a. Brainstorm, create goals for your collective or your grow
   b. Research current local, county and state MMJ laws
   c. Pull together an operating team of qualified individuals (if applicable)
4. Choose an entity for your not-for-profit business
5. Create a collective or cooperative corporation (if applicable)
6. Begin to cultivate medical marijuana as a collective or cooperative:
   a. Ensure that everyone in your collective (or co-op) has a current doctor's medical marijuana recommendation
   b. Make sure members are aware that they are members/shareholders in the collective corporation
      i. Require that members provide more than just money for marijuana (i.e. donate time or goods to the collective)
   c. Keep detailed records of
      i. income and expenses
      ii. grow expenses and operations
      iii. time donated by members
   d. Ensure that all your medical marijuana is kept in a "closed loop" system, in which marijuana is cultivated by members and provided only to members (and never resold)

Overview

The ever-evolving medical marijuana industry has been around in California for over 15 years. Throughout this time, the industry has endured in an unclear legal atmosphere, and the interpretation and enforcement of laws vary widely from county to county. We, along with other medical marijuana advocates, hope that California will legalize this plant sooner rather than later. Unfortunately, every time we take a step forward toward legalization, we soon take one or two steps back. It is mandatory that you stay aware of current laws at the state, county, and city levels. Also, please be politically active and promote the positive aspects of marijuana whenever possible.

The medical marijuana industry has recently been described as the modern-day gold rush. Many people are eager to jump into the industry and, given all the positive press (and economic data), we don't blame them. In 2011, CNBC aired its *Marijuana, Inc.* documentary nationwide and has rebroadcast it repeatedly. This program showed people growing giant plants in Northern California with little fear of prosecution. However, don't be fooled; dozens of arrests are taking place every day, and there are still big risks involved with this industry.

California allows an exemption from prosecution if you are operating under specific rules, but it is important to remember that profits are not allowed in this industry. However, you can make a living wage by working as a dispensary director, employee, or grower. Given the loose regulations in place, some people are taking advantage, and you will need to work extra hard to separate yourself from the bad apples. A person can live very comfortably working within the California medical marijuana guidelines.

Chapter 1- Laws

As a starting point, we will outline the state and federal laws regarding medical marijuana. This legal chapter is first because the laws are the foundation for the usage of medical marijuana. It is extremely important that you understand and abide by all laws outlined below. Failure to abide by the state laws (and guidelines) will result in your medical marijuana exemption being disallowed, which will then render all your marijuana usage, possession, and cultivation illegal. Unfortunately, until the federal government acknowledges the benefits of medical marijuana, you will be susceptible to federal law violations.

Federal Law

The federal government still views marijuana as a Schedule 1 narcotic, on par with cocaine and heroin.

Adopted in 1970, the Controlled Substances Act (CSA) established a federal regulatory system designed to combat recreational drug abuse by making it unlawful to manufacture, distribute, dispense, or possess any controlled substance. (21 U.S.C. § 801, et seq.; *Gonzales v. Oregon* (2006) 546 U.S. 243, 271-273). The CSA reflects the federal government's view that marijuana is a drug with "no currently accepted medical use." (21 U.S.C. § 812(b) (1). Accordingly, the manufacture, distribution, or possession of marijuana is a federal criminal offense. (*Id.* at §§ 841(a) (1), 844(a)).

California's Medical Marijuana Laws

Proposition 215: The Compassionate Use Act, November 1996

On November 5, 1996, California voters passed Proposition 215, which decriminalized the cultivation and use of marijuana by seriously ill individuals upon a physician's recommendation. (§ 11362.5). Proposition 215 was enacted to "ensure that seriously ill Californians have the right to obtain and use marijuana for medical purposes where that medical use is deemed appropriate and has been recommended by a physician who has determined that the person's health would benefit from the use of marijuana," and to "ensure that patients and their primary caregivers who obtain and use marijuana for medical purposes upon the recommendation of a physician are not subject to criminal prosecution or sanction." (§ 11362.5(b) (1) (A)-(B)). [i]

The Act further states that "Section 11357, relating to the possession of marijuana, and Section 11358, relating to the cultivation of marijuana, shall not apply to a patient, or to a patient's primary caregiver, who possesses or cultivates marijuana for the personal medical purposes of the patient upon the written or verbal recommendation or approval of a physician." (§11362.5(d)). Courts have found an implied defense to the transportation of medical marijuana when the "quantity transported and the method, timing and distance of the transportation are reasonably related to the patient's current medical needs." (*People v. Trippet* (1997) 56 Cal.App.4th 1532, 1551).

Senate Bill 420: The Medical Marijuana Program Act (MMP), January 2004

On January 1, 2004, Senate Bill 420, the Medical Marijuana Program Act (MMP), became law. (§§ 11362.7-11362.83). The MMP, among other things, requires the California Department of Public Health (DPH) to establish and maintain a program for the voluntary registration of qualified medical marijuana patients and their primary caregivers through a statewide identification card system. Medical marijuana identification cards are intended to help law enforcement officers identify and verify that cardholders are able to cultivate, possess, and transport certain amounts of marijuana without being subject to arrest under specific conditions. (§§ 11362.71(e), 11362.78 ii).

This bill made it mandatory that all counties participate in the identification card program by (a) providing applications upon request to individuals seeking to join the identification card program; (b) processing completed applications; (c) maintaining certain records; (d) following state implementation protocols; and (e) issuing DPH identification cards to approved applicants and designated primary caregivers. (§ 11362.71(b)). Participation by patients and primary caregivers in the identification card program is voluntary. However, because identification cards offer the holder protection from arrest, are issued only after verification of the cardholder's status as a qualified patient or primary caregiver, and are immediately verifiable online or via telephone, they represent one of the best ways to ensure the security and non-diversion of marijuana grown for medical use.

In addition to establishing the identification card program, the MMP also defines certain terms, sets possession guidelines for cardholders, and recognizes a qualified right to collective and cooperative cultivation of medical marijuana. [ii]

From Senate Bill 420 to 2008

After SB 420 passed, we began to see more medical marijuana dispensaries begin to pop up throughout California, and things were going fairly smoothly. Certain cities took a more liberal approach and allowed dispensaries to flourish.

In the middle of 2007, a number of landlords in California received "advisory" letters from the DEA (under the Bush Administration) warning of the possibility of property forfeiture, and in a few instances U.S. Attorneys backed up the DEA letters with actual threats to file charges. Many property owners forced the dispensaries to close down, and the dispensary operators and their landlords who didn't close down weren't sleeping very soundly.

It wasn't until the 2008 presidential campaign that patients saw a glimmer of "hope" –Barack Obama made multiple comments during his campaign about his ideas regarding the proper allocation of scarce law enforcement resources. He said dispensaries operating in accord with California law would not be a priority for his administration and, based on these statements, patients believed that Obama was medical-marijuana friendly and a good presidential candidate (for the MMJ industry). Unfortunately, we were deceived – the Obama Administration has continued to attack medical marijuana providers. Please see Chapter 12 for more details.

Attorney General Jerry Brown Issues Medical Marijuana Guidelines (August 2008)

California Attorney General Jerry Brown published guidelines for qualified medical marijuana patients, providers and state law enforcement in August 2008. These guidelines provide information for medical marijuana patients and law enforcement on how to comply with California's current medical marijuana laws and are the most detailed information the State has provided. Unfortunately, these guidelines are not binding in court, but they do provide a foundation for law enforcement, district attorneys and judges.

It was a great step forward for the California medical marijuana industry when these guidelines were issued: This was the state's highest-ranking law enforcement official acknowledging that "a properly organized and operated collective or cooperative that dispenses medical marijuana through a storefront may be lawful under California law," if they followed the rules outlined. Unfortunately, these guidelines were too general and left too much room for interpretation (which we will discuss later). However, as of the printing of this book in July 2012, this is still the most pertinent document relating to medical marijuana compliance in California (See **Attachment 1**).

State Attorney General Kamala Harris Seeks Clarification (December 2011)

In late December of 2011, the California State Attorney General, Kamala Harris, issued a statement to California lawmakers urging them to clarify the state's medical marijuana laws. She pleaded with them to provide "substantive changes" that will clear up some of the ambiguity in the industry. She went on to state that the current laws are not clearly laid out for either law enforcement or medical marijuana patients. Harris pushed the burden back on the Legislature to provide this clarification, rather than revise her predecessor's 2008 medical marijuana guidelines. If the Legislature issues specific medical marijuana requirements, it would save a lot of the state's court time and resources.[iii]

Priority of Compliance

You will want to comply with all the legal rules from the state down to your local government. It is very important not to lose sight of how to prioritize the various agencies' (i.e., state, county, and city) regulations as they apply to medical marijuana. If your city allows dispensaries, it is very easy to get caught up in the local zoning issues and lose sight of the state guidelines that should carry the most weight and be your primary focus. You should, of course, be concerned with city operational requirements, but your first priority is to make sure you are operating under the state's medical exemption laws. It is much easier to fight a city violation about zoning issues (e.g., hours of operation or signage) than a criminal (state level) marijuana violation (which could include jail time and a criminal record). City violations typically show up in the mail and include small to moderate fines. We are hopeful that, at some point, the federal government will be at the top of the list, but for now there is no way to comply with them. Limiting the size of your organization and keeping it professional and compliant with the other agencies is your best bet for staying off the federal government's radar.

Unfortunately, the attorney general's guidelines are only 11 pages long and leave a lot of room for interpretation. You and everyone involved with your operation will need to study and understand the attorney general's guidelines. You will also need to review the material in this manual, do your own due diligence, consult an attorney, and stay current on all medical marijuana issues.

Chapter 2 - Becoming a Medical Marijuana Patient

To possess, use or grow medical marijuana in California, you need a doctor's recommendation. Once you have received a doctor's recommendation you can possess, use, grow marijuana, and be immune to the criminal violations normally associated with these activities if you abide by specific guidelines set up by the state.

Doctor's Recommendation to Use Medical Marijuana

The medical marijuana industry essentially starts with the doctors. A doctor can issue a "recommendation" to use marijuana for medical needs. These typed or written recommendations are similar to prescriptions and allow patients to be exempt from the regular state marijuana laws. Since marijuana cannot legally be prescribed by a physician or dispensed by a pharmacy per federal law, the best thing a doctor can do is issue their recommendation for use. Although a verbal recommendation is sufficient according to the law, a written document is required by collectives and may reduce your chances of being arrested. Even having an expired recommendation will provide you with a defense in court. However, it is recommended that anyone using medical marijuana have a current doctor's recommendation.

Prop 215, Health and Safety Code 11262.5, states that its purpose is "To ensure that seriously ill Californians have the right to obtain and use marijuana for medical purposes where that medical use is deemed appropriate and has been recommended by a physician who has determined that the person's health would benefit from the use of marijuana in the treatment of cancer, anorexia, AIDS, chronic pain, spasticity, glaucoma, arthritis, migraine, **or any other illness for which marijuana provides relief**." It is this last statement that allows doctors to be liberal in writing these recommendations. California Health and Safety Code 11362.7 specifically reads, "Any other chronic or persistent medical symptom that either: (A) Substantially limits the ability of the person to conduct one or more major life activities as defined in the Americans with Disabilities Act of 1990 (Public Law 101-336)." This code seems to provide a little more limitation on what qualifies as "other" acceptable illness. It is ultimately the doctor's decision on who qualifies for medical marijuana.

The People v. Spark (2004 California Court of Appeals) is a pertinent case that states that a jury cannot second-guess a doctor's recommendation for a patient who is seriously ill, because a person's medical condition is confidential. This provided patients and doctors with more protection from prosecution.

As discussed earlier, Senate Bill 420 initiated a statewide program for the voluntary registration of qualified medical marijuana patients through an identification card system. Under this program, local counties (via the Department of Health) must issue state ID cards that verify your recommendation to use medical marijuana. The county will verify with the recommending doctor that your recommendation is valid, take a photo, and have the card produced in a few weeks. These ID cards don't provide any more protection than the regular doctor's recommendation, although there are a few advantages to having a state-issued card: It is official, and it will likely hold more weight for local law enforcement, since they don't need to contact your doctor to verify your recommendation letter (which could easily be forged or replicated). There is a web site where these state-issued ID cards can be verified. The cost for these state IDs is currently about $166 and can vary from county to county. Medi-Cal recipients will receive a 50% fee reduction. The state portion of the fee is $66.00, and the counties add their $100 administration fees.

Doctor's Exam/Interview

Prepare for the conversation you are going to have with the doctor ahead of time. What ailments do you have that are improved by the use of medical marijuana? Research your condition before you go to your appointment. You should plan ahead and have a list of questions that you would like answered. The typical appointment won't last very long, so it is good to be prepared and take advantage of your time with the doctor. Educate yourself about your medical condition and research what benefits cannabis can provide. In addition, certain strains of medical marijuana are likely to be more helpful in treating certain conditions. Start building a foundation of knowledge so that you can seek the most suitable treatments and better your life.

Doctors often recommend a set number of plants that can be grown or a given quantity of dried marijuana that can be possessed (i.e. 12 immature or 6 mature plants, or 8 ounces of marijuana). Some doctors are more knowledgeable and can provide more specific recommendations on the amount of cannabis that should be grown by an individual, based on personal consumption and grow methods. For example, If a patient plans to obtain their year's worth of medicine from a single outdoor grow, they would require a significantly higher quantity allowance compared to a patient who wants to join a collective and not personally grow his or her own marijuana.

Most doctors will have you fill out a medical history form before starting the exam. They will then take your vital signs and perform a brief physical. If pain is your issue, the doctor might ask you what your pain level is (on a level from 1-10) without the use of marijuana and then when you are medicated. The doctor will also ask about other medications you take and past experiences with marijuana. You should feel comfortable telling the doctor that you currently use marijuana and that it helps with your medical (or psychological) condition. Most doctors are sympathetic to people who are looking for alternatives to addictive pharmaceutical drugs.

You may end up with a doctor who wants to keep detailed records of his patients and why he feels marijuana is appropriate. Some doctors will want to get copies of past medical records, e.g., MRI or x-ray records, or a diagnosis from a specialist or primary physician. The doctors will also briefly describe the state laws and how best to comply. There is no reason to be nervous at your appointment; relax and enjoy this process that opens the gates to the world of medical marijuana.

In the last five years, the number of doctors that will write recommendations has increased dramatically. Fortunately, the increase in the number of marijuana doctors has brought down the price for exams and/or recommendations. Also, the doctor's recommendation will likely be written on the spot that day. A typical recommendation is good for one year; however, some doctors offer shorter durations for discounted rates. In most large cities, these doctors are competitively marketing to patients. Some doctors will advertise a low base rate that will later be increased before you receive your recommendation, so be sure to confirm all the fees associated with the recommendation before you make an appointment. Depending on your location, you should expect to pay anywhere from $80- $150 for a one-year recommendation. The price is also often discounted for those renewing a recommendation.

Some doctors will try to up-sell ID cards and other miscellaneous items. However, their ID card serves no real purpose and should not be confused with the state-issued ID cards (under SB420). Most dispensaries will not accept the ID cards and will still require that you present your original, signed (and often embossed) recommendation letter.

Chapter 3 - Opportunities for Employment/ (Reasonable) Compensation

Growing Medical Marijuana vs. Running a Collective

There are two direct ways to become involved in the California medical marijuana industry: operate a collective, or grow medical marijuana. These two activities are intertwined and require each other to survive. It is possible to do both of these activities, but keep in mind that your time is limited, and you will likely have to determine what you are more interested in doing and which activity your skills are best suited for. In general, growing medical marijuana is much simpler than organizing and running a collective, which requires following a number of regulations while handling all the headaches of a typical medical office/retail store.

Growing requires spending a lot of time alone with the plants, while running a collective is a much more social endeavor and requires a lot of face time with patients. You will need to weigh the pros and cons to determine where you see the best fit for yourself. After reading this book, you should have a much better understanding of what is required for either of these activities.

Advantages of Growing	Advantages of Running a Collective
Easy start-up	Potential for higher compensation
More flexibility and freedom	Provide patients with medicine/relief
Lower start-up funds required	Provide jobs for the community
Solitary working environment	Social working environment

There are also a number of opportunities to work at or for a collective; typical positions include clerical, accounting, green room tender, and on-site medical marijuana expert. Depending on the size of the collective, one person might be responsible for a number of duties.

Dispensary and Collective Explained

A dispensary is a physical location, often a storefront, where medical marijuana is distributed and, per Wikipedia.org, "a **collective** is a group of entities that share or are motivated by at least one common issue or interest, or work together on a specific project(s) to achieve a common objective." A dispensary is a meeting place, such as a club house (or Moose Lodge),_where members can meet. A collective is an entity composed of people working together, which can exist with or without a physical location. A medical marijuana collective is a group of people who bond together to cultivate and obtain marijuana for medical needs. Typically, a storefront location is chosen by a collective's board of directors, because this is the best, most efficient way to serve its members. Alternatives to a dispensary include meeting at various members' homes to distribute medical marijuana or delivering it to each other.

An individual/sole proprietor could open a dispensary (to sell medical marijuana) without being part of a collective. However, this is illegal under California law. We will discuss later how to properly form and operate a collective (corporation) in California; there are specific characteristics this organization must have. Also, assume that cooperatives and collectives are the same, and we will discuss both these entities in greater detail in the next chapter.

Chapter 4 – Planning and Incorporating as a Collective c to Provide MMJ to Members

Planning and Organization

What are your goals?

You will want a written plan that outlines your ideas and goals. Depending on where you plan to open your collective, you might need to provide a business and operating plan to the city as part of their application process. You can create an outline for yourself and a more detailed version for the city or other outside parties. If you are opening a low profile delivery service, your outline will not require as much detail.

Brainstorming

Write down all your ideas without considering whether they are good or bad; you will refine your list later. What do you want, and how are you going to get there?

Create a mission statement for your organization

A **mission statement** is a short, written statement of the purpose of the organization. This will be a necessity for a collective, and although not needed for cultivators, it isn't a bad idea to document your passion and make goals for yourself. This statement should summarize the objectives/core values of the club into a few short sentences, such as "To provide the highest quality of medicinal products and services to our members while supporting local charities." Spend some time researching non-profit business to help you get a better understanding of a mission statement. You will find that a lot of information is available online.

Choosing and Creating an Entity

Per the California Attorney General's Guidelines:

Under California law, medical marijuana patients and primary caregivers may "associate within the State of California in order <u>collectively</u> or <u>cooperatively</u> to cultivate marijuana for medical purposes." (§11362.775). The following guidelines are meant to apply to qualified patients and primary caregivers who come together in order to collectively or cooperatively cultivate (physician-recommended) medical marijuana.

Business Forms: Any group that is (a) collectively or (b) cooperatively cultivating and distributing marijuana for medical purposes should be organized and operated in a manner that ensures the security of the crop and safeguards against diversion for non-medical purposes."

The attorney general's guidelines were developed to help cooperatives and collectives operate within the law, and to help law enforcement determine whether they are doing so.

(a.) Collective

"A collective is a group of entities that share or are motivated by at least one common issue or interest, or work together on a specific project(s) to achieve a common objective".[iv] When you hear most people talk about a collective, it will either be an incorporated entity, such as a mutual benefit corporation (which requires incorporating with the State of California), or a less structured collective association (or unincorporated nonprofit association). California law also allows for the creation of a consumer collective corporation.

(b.) Cooperative (Co-op)

A cooperative is a "union of individuals, commonly laborers, farmers, or small capitalists, formed for the prosecution in common of some productive enterprise, the profits being shared in accordance with the capital or labor contributed by each." (164 N.W. 804, 805.) There are no specific requirements for incorporating or being acknowledged by the state. A cooperative can be incorporated or organized as an LLC, S-Corp, or C-Corp, but it is not required to do so (similar to a collective association). Cooperative corporations are "democratically controlled and are not organized to make a profit for themselves, as such, or for their members, as such, but primarily for their members as patrons." (Id. at § 12201.) [v] [vi]

The purpose of these entities is basically the same – to come together to grow and obtain medical marijuana. As noted, you can register these entities with the state or take the less-regulated route and not incorporate. The advantage of incorporating is that the members will not be personally liable for loss or damages, and they can more easily open bank accounts and perform other business-related activities. Profiting from medical marijuana is not legal in California, regardless of the entity you choose to use.

Nonprofit mutual benefit corporation(C-Corp)

In our opinion, the best entity for forming a collective dispensary is a nonprofit/not-for-profit mutual benefit corporation. A mutual benefit corporation is a corporation that is set up for the sole benefit of its members. These nonprofit corporations should not seek tax exemption under IRS code section 501 (we explain this in more detail later in this chapter). If this type of corporation did generate a profit, it would be taxed, but generally profits are given back to the members, used (or reserved) for general improvements or overall member benefit. (We owe credit in choosing this entity to Gene Takagi, who is an extremely smart, friendly lawyer based in San Francisco, CA.)

There isn't one "correct" entity for forming a dispensary or collective. Some attorneys will disagree with the mutual benefit corporation choice and may prefer a cooperative or collective association entity. A variety of these entities will work just fine—it really comes down to the operations of the business and the intentions of the founding members. There are a number of operational requirements a mutual benefit corporation must follow to remain compliant with state law, and these will provide guidance to the collective's operations. A mutual benefit corporation will provide protection for the board of directors and management by placing attaching liabilities to the corporation, instead of to the individuals. This structure also allows the collective to carry out the functions of a regular business (i.e., opening bank accounts, employing workers and properly filing payroll taxes, filing annual income tax returns, etc.).

If you are running a low-key delivery service, you might be able to function under one of the less-regulated entity structures. Some organizations form these alternative types of entities hoping to draw less attention to themselves (and to try to stay below the radar of various state agencies). Obtain professional legal advice from an attorney who specializes in these entities, and document the thought and creation process.

Primary Caregiver

A **primary caregiver** is a person who is designated by a qualified patient and "has consistently assumed responsibility for the housing, health, or safety" of the patient (§ 11362.5(e)). This model isn't applicable for most medical marijuana providers unless they meet the strict definition provided.

The highly instrumental case that addressed the caregiver model was *People v. Mentch* (California Supreme Court, Nov. 24, 2008). It was decided that caregivers need to be doing more than just providing medicine. The California Supreme Court held that a person is not a "primary caregiver" under the Compassionate Use Act merely because they are in charge of getting someone's marijuana. Given that "primary caregiver" is defined in the statute as "the individual . . . who has consistently assumed responsibility for the housing, health, or safety of that person," this decision isn't all that surprising. Providing medical marijuana doesn't necessarily mean that you've undertaken the responsibility for a person's "housing, health, or safety," much less that you've done so on a consistent basis.

That determination is all that the California Supreme Court needed to decide this case. But it went further, and the Court unanimously held that not only does a "primary caregiver" under the Compassionate Use Act have to be what we might traditionally call a primary caregiver, but further held that this relationship must also have been commenced at or before the provision of medical marijuana. The Court stated: "[W]e conclude a defendant asserting primary caregiver status must prove at a minimum that he or she (1) consistently provided care giving, (2) independent of any assistance in taking medical marijuana, (3) at or before the time he or she assumed responsibility for assisting with medical marijuana." [vii]

Nonprofits, Not-for-Profits, and 501(c)(3) Organizations

Nonprofit and not-for-profit can, for the most part, be used interchangeably; the real differences arise when an organization receives tax-exempt status. When most people think of nonprofits, they are referring to 501(c)(3) tax-exempt organizations that derive the bulk of their funding through charitable contributions. For example, the budgets of the American Cancer Society, Operation Smile or the Catholic Church down the street come through contributions. 501(c)(3) organizations are tax-exempt, nonprofit corporations or associations that meet specific criteria and apply for exemption with the IRS. There are various types of tax-exempt organizations recognized by the IRS (with 501(c)(3) being the most common). There is no legal distinction between nonprofit and not-for-profit; both can qualify as a tax-exempt organization under the U.S. Tax Code. The difference between tax-exempt and non-tax-exempt is the organization's business models and sources of operating funds.

A medical marijuana collective typically does not qualify as a 501(c)(3) tax-exempt organization and should not seek that status. 501(c)(3)'s have more complicated tax and regulatory requirements that would be difficult to comply with. However, a properly run collective won't owe taxes, since it doesn't make a profit (and runs at a break-even or slight deficit). Again, the 501(c)(3) federal designation isn't advised for medical marijuana entities.

A nonprofit or not-for-profit collective derives its funding from operating a business. It provides a service—in this case, producing and providing herbal medicine—as a charity and charges just enough to cover operating expenses. Very commonly, these businesses offer a sliding scale, with those less able to pay being charged less than cost, and those able to pay more making up the difference. You can also vary the cost to members based on the number of members using the service (i.e., prices go down as membership goes up).

The main issue for both types of not-for-profit entities is that no profits or dividends are removed from the organization. If the entity makes a profit during any period, (realistically, one year), this excess must be returned to members or put back into the organization, such as by capital improvements or charitable donations based on the will of the members. The best way to determine the use of excess income is by member's vote. As long as management/officers' wages remain "reasonable," they can be increased by the board. Be sure you document the rationale for any raises and bonuses given, and please pay special attention to this. Your local ordinance might restrict the use of bonuses; for example, the city of Santa Barbara Ordinance #5526 states, "The payment of a bonus shall not be considered reasonable compensation" and is thus not allowed.

Incorporating (as a mutual benefit corporation)

Incorporating any entity in California is done through the office of the Secretary of State. Although these instructions are specific to a mutual benefit corporation, the basic steps will be very similar for the incorporation of other entities.

1. Choose who will be on the original board of directors (BOD)
   i. What is the business address?

    ii. Who will be the corporation's agent for service? An agent for service of process is the individual designated by a corporation or limited liability company to accept tax notifications and legal papers for the business. The agent must deliver these documents to the owners of the business promptly. This person can be a board member, attorney, or other responsible party.[viii]

2. Choose a name for the Collective
   i. Although your mutual benefit corporation is a collective, you aren't required to use "collective" in the name. For instance, Green Mountain Collective can be just "Green Mountain" because it *is* a collective. Not using the word "collective" will possibly help keep your organization off the radar, to some degree, and is recommended.
   ii. Verify that the corporate name you want is available by searching the California Secretary of State's website (http://kepler.sos.ca.gov/), which is a database of all the entities registered with the state of California.

3. File your Articles of Incorporation
   i. This is a simple one-page information sheet that must be typed.
      1. Very specific wording is required by California law: "This Corporation is a nonprofit mutual benefit corporation organized under the Nonprofit Mutual Benefit Corporation Law. The purpose of this corporation is to engage in any lawful act or activity, other than credit union business, for which a corporation may be organized under such law." [ix]
   ii. Item B – "The specific purpose of this corporation is to _____".
      1. This statement provides the specific purpose of the corporation. This statement can be brief and left very broad. Be creative; this is the organization's opportunity to highlight alternative services offered by your collective (which could be very beneficial to avoid IRS Section 280 issues which we will discuss later (Chapter 8).
      2. Examples
         a. "Provide members with natural health products."
         b. "Provide alternative forms of medicine."
         c. "Meet the holistic medical needs of its members."
   iii. See **Attachment 2** for an example.

4. Create bylaws for your corporation.
   i. Bylaws are the rules that outline the operations of the organization, setting out the form, manner or procedure in which the organization should be run. Corporate bylaws are drafted by a corporation's founders or directors under the authority of its Articles of Incorporation.[x]

ii. These bylaws will provide the detailed rules of the collective. It should incorporate many of the ideas that were developed in the planning process. The bylaws need to comply with California law and contain the rules and procedures your corporation will follow for holding meetings, electing officers and directors, and taking care of other corporate formalities required in California. The more detail in the bylaws, the better. These form the core legal structure for your organization. [xi]

> It is best that the board of directors be voted on by the members. You want the members to choose the board of director/oversight committee, as this is a democratic entity. Think of a collective in the traditional sense of the word, where decisions should ultimately be made to benefit the majority of the members.

5. Hold your first official board of directors meeting
   i. Be sure you have written minutes documenting all items discussed; the secretary of your organization should sign and date all minutes.
      1. Approve the bylaws.
      2. Appoint the officers who will run day-to-day operations.
      3. Verify the accounting period (typically December 31st as year end).
      4. Acknowledge that the corporation can begin operating.
      5. Set up a corporate binder that will hold all of the recently created legal documents. All items (e.g., minutes) should be filed and kept on-site. [xii]

View the California Corporations Code for more information.
http://www.leginfo.ca.gov/.html/corp_table_of_contents.html

Corporate Compliance

As the founder of a mutual benefit corporation, you are required to hold members' and directors' meetings, maintain corporate records, and document major corporate decisions. If you neglect these formalities and your collective runs into legal trouble, a court may decide to disregard your corporate status—and hold you personally responsible for the collective's debts or even disallow your medical exception for marijuana. [xiii]

The collective is required to have a formal annual members' meeting as outlined in the bylaws. It is recommended that the collective hold member meetings more often, such as quarterly, to stay in closer contact with the members. A meeting can be held at any time throughout the year as along as members are given proper notice. All BOD meetings should be documented and stored in the collective's corporate binder. An example of items that would be voted on at the annual members' meeting would be:

1. Removing a director without cause
2. Filling vacancies on the board
3. Amending the bylaws or Articles of Incorporation
4. Electing to make a large capital/asset purchase

Statement of Information (filed with the California Secretary of State)

- This Statement of Information, Form (SI-100), is required when incorporating. Every **domestic nonprofit, credit union and consumer cooperative corporation** must file a Statement of Information with the California Secretary of State, within 90 days after filing of the initial Articles of Incorporation, and biannually **(every other year)** thereafter. This form is available on the California Secretary of State's website.

- The purpose of the form is to provide the state with current information on the collective (i.e., location and management details).

- The main item on the Statement of Information asks about the three officer positions within the corporation; your corporation will need a management team of three positions as a minimum requirement of the State of California: chief executive officer (CEO), chief financial officer (CFO), and secretary. These positions can all be filled by the same person, but that is not recommended, especially if there isn't a separate board of directors overseeing operations.

- See **Attachment 3** for a blank copy. Also available at the Secretary of State's website.
  http://www.sos.ca.gov/business/corp/pdf/so/corp_so100.pdf

- Failure to file will result in a $50 penalty.

- Note in the Incorporating section #4 above that an individual can hold all of the officer positions, if this is allowed by the bylaws.

Obtaining an Employee Identification Number (EIN)

This is a federal identification number that is different from the California corporation (or other entity) number obtained from the Secretary of State upon incorporation. "This EIN is your permanent number and can be used immediately for most of your business needs, including opening a bank account, applying for business licenses, and filing a tax return by mail. However, no matter how you apply (phone, fax, mail, or online), it will take up to two weeks before your EIN becomes part of the IRS' permanent records. You must wait until this occurs before you can file an electronic return, make an electronic payment, or pass an IRS Taxpayer Identification Number matching program."

- An EIN can be obtained by phone, online or by mail.

- Taxpayers can obtain an EIN immediately by calling the Business & Specialty Tax Line at (800) 829-4933. The hours of operation are 7:00 a.m. - 10:00 p.m. local time, Monday through Friday

- Online is probably the easiest method – their website is www.irs.gov

Creating a Not-for-Profit Business Plan

1. Executive Summary

   a. This section should be a concise overview of the entire plan, along with summary information about the directors/founders. This section tells your reader who you are, the current circumstances of the organization, and where you want it to be. (This will have some crossover from the vision statement).

2. Market Analysis

   a. Specific research should be done on the specific market you will operate in. Who needs your services, and what competitive organizations will you face? This section should outline your knowledge about the medical marijuana industry and where you will fit in.

3. Organization and Management

   a. This contains the organizational structure and outlines how the organization will function. It should provide background on the founders and what skills they bring to the organization. This section should also detail each position in the organization and associated responsibilities.

   b. Determine who can fill the various Board of Director and management positions. Develop a list of ideal qualities for vacant positions.

4. Operations

   a. This section should contain a broad description of how your organization is going to function. Outline the nature of your organization and list the primary factors that you believe will make your organization a success. Identify the marketplace needs that you are trying to satisfy and detail the ways in which you plan to satisfy these needs.

5. Products/Services

   a. A detailed description of your products and services, including the products and services available to members. You should include specific items that will attract new members to your collective: What non-marijuana products and services will be available?

6. Marketing/Member Recruitment

   a. How are you going to reach potential members? Typically, this section consists of public relations, personal promotion, social networks, and printed materials. Once you have defined your membership goals, develop a marketing strategy to match. You will constantly need to evaluate your efforts (e.g., questioning new patients). Please be careful about how you present your collective to the public.

   b. As of the last election, more than 50% of the public voted against legalization of marijuana and likely aren't 420-friendly. With that being said, produce professional-looking ads and focus more on helping patients with their medical needs. Make sure any advertising clearly states that your organization is fully compliant with SB 420 and prop 215.

7. Funding

    a. Who is going to fund the start-up costs of your collective? Outline the funds needed to get the collective running and cover operating expenses for a few months (until reimbursements can cover expenses). Please refer to the budget section for more detail. Although it is best to fund your operations internally (through member investors), you may need to seek funding from outside investors. This is something you will need to discuss with your attorney before any funding takes place. No equity/ownership can be associated with these loans, and the terms and interest rate of the loan should be defendable. (As a side note, if you form a cooperative corporation, you have the ability to issue preferred shares to members who can pay a given rate of interest. The rate of return is limited by law, and these payments must be paid routinely, which can make using this funding option difficult.)

You most likely won't have a lot of information to plug into all seven items listed above. Instead, focus on your experience and background as well as the decisions that led you to start this particular entity. Include information about the problems your target market has and what solutions you provide. Show how the expertise you have will allow you to make significant inroads into the market. Describe your goals, and convince people to jump aboard with you.

Create a Vision Statement

Organizations can also benefit by creating a vision statement. A **vision statement** is a picture of your future endeavor (grow or collective), but more than that, your vision statement is your inspiration, the structure for all you're planning to do. The vision statement is typically more detailed and focused on future goals than the closely related mission statement. A vision statement may apply to you alone or to the entire collective. Whether for all or part of an organization, the vision statement answers the question, "Where do we want to go?" What you are doing in creating a vision statement is recording your dreams and hopes for your business. This way, you can regularly go back to your original vision and make sure you are staying on the right track. While a vision statement doesn't tell you how you're going to get there, it does set the basis for your operation planning. When crafting a vision statement, you should use your imagination and dream big. You should map out your ideal situation – it contains your passion for starting. The mission statement and your core competencies can be a valuable starting point for articulating your values. This statement should also document where you see your project years from now. Your vision statement should have an influence on decision-making starting on day one and help with your allocation of resources. Unfortunately, you need to keep in mind that there is the potential for law enforcement and the court to read this statement, so be smart when you create it.

Remember, in creating your vision statement, be sure to address this question: How can your operation be better than any others you have seen?

Getting a Mentor

Ideally, you already know someone in the medical marijuana business who you can ask for advice. Cities develop various zoning requirements, and having a successful mentor is priceless. The more people you can bring together to help with the formation of your entity, the better it will be in the end. It is important that everyone understands their role in the dispensary, so be sure to document any founders or board positions right off the bat. You don't want to have anyone feel that they were taken advantage of or led on down the road.

Create bonds within the MMJ community

Have discussions with other collectives and create a coalition in the community. The more people you have working together, the greater your organization will become. You can never have too much knowledge, and new perspectives can be very helpful.

Gathering a Team

It's best not to go at this venture alone; your likelihood of success will be much greater if you can put together a team of qualified individuals. You probably already have a group of friends or associates who would help you create this entity. Remember, you can always start small and bring on new management members as needed. The size of your collective will also determine how much assistance you will require. Also, keep in mind that many cities require background checks for anyone involved with a collective, and, in general, individuals with felony convictions won't be allowed to work in (or open) a collective. Be sure you verify your particular circumstances with your local government.

Local Politics

The location of your collective will have a lot to do with how you operate: Some cities are much more liberal and accepting of collective dispensaries. You will need to do your research to determine how your local politicians feel about medical marijuana. In some instances, it may be best to befriend the mayor or a few city council members, and even some local police. On the other hand, in some instances it is better to keep your beliefs to yourself. By attending city council and other local government meetings, you should be able to determine which side people will lean toward with regard to medical marijuana. You are better off solidifying relationships with pro-medical marijuana politicians than attempting to convert the others. Attending these meetings will also keep you active and up to date with your local government issues. In some cities, you will be fighting an uphill battle, and your only option will be to create a clandestine delivery-style collective. Nothing is fool-proof, but having the right contacts can provide you with a greater sense of security.

Community Support

In order to create a successful organization, you will need allies. Only a certain percentage of the population needs medical marijuana, and you will want to make friends with as many neighbors and non-patients as possible so they can support your cause. Do your part to make your environment a better, happier place. As an active medical marijuana provider or grower, you represent the larger MMJ community. We need to work toward changing the negative stereotypes that a minority has created over the years.

Hiring an Attorney

Anyone involved in medical marijuana should have a relationship with an attorney who deals with marijuana-related business. Oftentimes, attorneys will specialize or focus on either compliance or criminal defense. A compliance attorney will typically focus on planning, incorporation, and teaching clients to maintain their legal status, while a criminal attorney will focus on getting you out of trouble after an arrest. Some attorneys will serve both functions or will partner with another attorney who specializes in the other area. Do your research and find someone you feel comfortable with. Also, negotiate fees up front so there are no complications or misunderstandings down the road.

A compliance lawyer will be needed to help draft bylaws, file incorporating documents, and create membership and grower agreements. With the help of this book, you should be able to handle all of these items yourself, but it is recommended that you seek the advice of an attorney who can better address your specific circumstances.

A criminal attorney should also be lined up in case you or a member of your collective is arrested. You need to think of the worst-case scenario and have an emergency plan in order, which should include having money set aside to use for bail. Ideally, you will have enough money set aside to post bail, pay for an attorney and provide for a few months of living expenses. Oftentimes the police will seize ALL of an individual's liquid assets (with a cultivation or sales arrest), so be sure to have an emergency account or cash to be held in trust by a family member.

Chapter 5 - Opening a Storefront Dispensary

After the formation and legal matters (discussed in Chapter 4) have been covered, you can then turn your attention to the financial and operational aspects of your business. Many of the fundamental aspects of this chapter will also apply to the delivery service model.

Create a Budget

Brainstorm about all potential expenses you expect the organization to have. If you have been involved with your own business before, you should have a good idea of the general business expenses that will be required.

Using spreadsheet software, such as Microsoft Excel, will help you keep your budget flexible so you can periodically make changes as more information becomes available.

Start-up capital required: Ideally, the business will have enough cash/funding available to pay for:

i. Building changes/tenant improvements required to the dispensary location, furniture, security systems, computers, reinforced doors, bulletproof glass, etc.
ii. Attorney fees or retainer.
iii. Cash reserves to cover expenses for a few months of operation (see below). This cash reserve or available line of credit will help you sleep much easier at night.
iv. Typically, funding can be a major factor in keeping people from starting any venture. It is possible to open up with a shoe-string budget; however, thinking ahead and securing people with back-up funding will not be a waste of time. It is better to over-insure yourself with a back-up source of funds, as unexpected problems are inevitable.

Sales projections

For sales estimates, you can estimate the average number of patients you plan to see per day and average the purchase per patient. For example, 30 patients per day, with an average purchase of one-eighth at $40 is 30x$40 = $1,200 a day or $1,200 x 30 days = $36,000 in revenue or reimbursement per month.

Fixed vs. variable expenses

- Fixed costs are your monthly costs that remain the same each month. An example is rent or insurance expense.
- Variable costs would be the medicine or to-go bags used, which can vary month to month depending on the activity of the business.

COGS, or cost of goods sold is the cost involved in producing the medicine.

Estimate your COGS as a percentage of sales. For example, COGS at 40% sales would leave 60% of sales going to cover the other operating expenses; with $100 for a ¼ ounce, $40 was spent to grow the product, and $60 covers all other expenses. (See Excel Spreadsheet – **Attachment 4.**)

The collective's medicine can come from two sources:

    i. The collective management can produce its own product
    ii. Members can grow medicine for the collective

Operating Expenses: These are the expenses associated with doing business, and they cover a wide range of topics. Operating expenses are covered in more detail in Chapter 8 - Day to Day Operations.

- Rent
- Utilities
- Electric, water, trash, Internet, alarm
- You will typically need to set up accounts with the various service providers (unless this is covered by your lease).
- Employees
    - i. Payroll tax (Chapter 9)
    - ii. Workers Compensation Insurance
    - iii. Using member volunteers to supplement paid employees
- Insurance
- Advertising
- Supplies

Finding a Location for a Dispensary

City Zoning

Zoning laws vary from city to city. It is very important that you fully understand your city's or county's position on medical marijuana. Do your research and due diligence by viewing your city's website and search past city council documents. Contact the local planning department and see what steps need to be taken. Even in a small town, it is highly unlikely that you will be the first person seeking this information.

Cities that allow dispensaries will typically require a permit (via an application process) and very specific operating requirements, such as: dispensaries must be located at least 1,000 feet from schools, churches, or other dispensaries. If no formal process has been developed, inquiries need to be made to city officials, and be sure to document all correspondence. Keep records of who you spoke with, where, when and why.

Not-for-profit delivery services are much harder for cities to regulate and are typically not addressed. It is difficult, if not illegal, for the city to restrict people from forming a collective group; however, please be aware that local law enforcement can still arrest you and run you through the court system. Please see Chapter 11 - Delivery Service for more details.

Business License

Many cities require a license before you can start a business within the city. Search your city's or county's website or call them for information. Business licenses typically have an annual fee based on the number of employees or the amount of revenue earned.

Generally, a business license won't be required for a delivery-style collective. However, please check with a local attorney before operating. It is best to have a prepared, professional answer for why you don't need a license. This may not get you out of all situations, but at least it shows you have done some homework and are trying to work within the system.

Physical location

The location of the collective is very important for your membership retention, security and overall success. First, you need to determine that the location is legal. You will want to make sure it is not near a school or church of any kind. These requirements vary city to city, but it is typically a 1,000-foot minimum. You will need to make sure the location is safe and secure for both the employees and the patients.

Unfortunately, marijuana dispensaries are still stereotyped as being shady businesses. Although the economy is currently in a lull and rental prices should generally be down, be aware that landlords often try to increase rental rates on dispensary tenants, and the recent federal threat has given them more leverage. However, don't accept substandard facilities or let the landlord push you around. You might need to be more flexible, given your circumstances, but just be aware of this going into negotiations—don't settle for an unfair deal. You don't want to be forced into a contract you will later regret. If things start out on the wrong foot, they will only get worse as time goes on. Once you have made needed tenant improvements and invested in the space, it will be harder for you to make a location change. You want to be up front with the landlord and create an open relationship (if possible).

Security & Collective Floor Plan

Security Measures

Dispensaries should have the functionality of a bank with the feel of a medical facility. With a secure, well-run dispensary, there shouldn't be a need for security guards because the collective is secured with the items outlined below. With proper procedures in place, you can avoid problems through the use of preventive measures.

- *Cameras* - You should have a system of eight to ten cameras that can be strategically placed throughout the collective. Systems are available online at Amazon or eBay for around $500, and these should be sufficient. You want to make sure the video is being recorded/backed up for at least a week. You should make a habit of testing the system frequently, as the last thing you want is to have an incident occur and not get it caught on tape. Getting the videos backed up off-site is even better if you have the capability.

- *Alarm system* - You will want to install a 24-hour security system that will detect any break-ins at the location, using a combination of glass breakage sensors and motion detectors. A company like ADT should be sufficient and will be able to consult with you on your various options. When an alarm is triggered, the security company will call the dispensary's first point of contact (e.g., the manager). If the first call isn't answered, or if a break-in is suspected by the first contact, the security company will then call the police.

- *Electronic door* - This will allow the employees to buzz in patients without needing to get up from the desk.

Security glass - Get high quality security glass with a paper slot at the bottom, similar to what you find at a bank. These are available for around $1,000 online.

Waiting room

This is the area for patients and non-patients to wait, fill out paperwork, etc. This room will be the first impression for people as they enter the collective, so keep this room clean and professional looking. You should have some medical marijuana reading material available, but no samples or other medical products. Americans for Safe Access sells a series of handbooks that provide information on cannabis usage to treat various health issues, and that would be an appropriate selection.

Restroom

Typically, a restroom will be required for employees, if not for patients as well. This will be dependent on your city's ordinances and personal preference.

Dispensing Area

The dispensary will need a menu board that can be easily modified. The menu will often be changing on a daily basis as medicines are moving through the dispensary. Typically, medicine is available in the following units: grams, 1/8 ounce, ¼ ounce, ½ ounce, or 1 ounce. Concentrates are typically sold in ½ grams or grams. Shake, joints, and edibles are also typical products that you will have available and can be listed on a supplementary menu or with the main menu. You can also get creative on how to present your menu; some collectives use chalk boards or dry eraser boards, while some choose flat screen televisions or computer monitors.

The dispensary can also run periodic or ongoing specials, but please be careful in the wording of your current specials. It doesn't look good when the dispensary appears to be or functions as a typical retail store instead of a medical dispensary.

For security and to utilize space efficiently, you will probably want to have a limited quantity of each strain available in the greenroom; two to three ounces of each strain should be sufficient. This will serve as your active inventory, from which you will take grams and smaller quantities. These storage containers can be glass or plastic; just make sure they are airtight to keep the medicine fresh. Glass mason jars work well, but they don't stack well and can take up a lot of space. There are some high quality plastic Tupperware products that also do the trick.

Make sure to verify with your local regulators the maximum allowable purchase per member, per day. This will typically be between 2 and 8 ounces. If someone purchases a large amount of medicine, they shouldn't be back for a while. It would be a good idea to make notes in the patients' files to ensure that they aren't buying large quantities very often. Please remember that diversion of medical marijuana to non-patients is illegal and will likely find its way back to the source— and you don't want to be that source.

The dispensary should have samples of all the strains for the patients to see. Typically you will have one nice-sized bud of each strain in a small jar for patients to review. Although not required, it is nice to allow the patients to touch and smell the product. This allows them to get the best sense of the product (short of smoking it).

The dispensary should have a decent amount of shake (small, loose pieces of bud) that is naturally created from day-to-day operations. Shake can be sold as is for smoking and cooking; however, the dispensary will be able to make use of a lot more if it's rolled and ready to smoke. A good basic joint will contain between 0.8 and 1 grams of shake. The best idea is to keep the A+ (Kush) shake separate from your average shake. This will allow the collective to recoup more (i.e. $8, versus $5) for the "grade A" joints. It's a good idea to ask growers to donate shake, or provide it at a significant discount, to the collective. Every employee should be rolling a set number of joints every day or week that will be available for purchase. If a procedure isn't put in place, it is highly unlikely that this will be done consistently. There isn't a good reason not to have these available at all times. Consistent sales of joints and shake will help the dispensary cover its expenses and keep patients happy.

Storage

A large safe is required to store the medicine overnight. One large, heavy-duty gun safe should provide more than enough room; ideally, this will be secured to the floor. It is best to keep the bulk of the medicine in the locked safe throughout the day, because, should you be robbed, it is much better to make access to the marijuana as difficult as possible.

Ideally, you will have a second, hidden floor safe (cemented in) for large amounts of cash, where periodic drops should be made to reduce the cash in the register. If you don't have a separate floor safe, keep the cash locked in the large safe with the medicine. Excess cash that will not be needed in the short term should be taken off-site.

Creating an Emergency Plan

Unfortunately, given the gray area of this industry, you will need to plan for multiple "emergency" situations that could arise due to your involvement with medical marijuana. You should be aware that until marijuana is legal on a federal level, there is no way to ensure that you won't be arrested or your organization or grow get shut down, for one reason or another, by local or federal law enforcement. If you are running a collective, illegal activities by members could negatively affect you. Criminals see medical marijuana growers and providers as easy targets, so you need to be extra cautious with everything you do. Member employees need to be made aware of these potential risks before they are hired. Everyone working or volunteering on-site needs to be prepared for one of the following situations:

- The collective being raided by local police
- The collective being raided by federal agents
- The collective or grow being robbed
- The arrest of a member grower
- The arrest of a patient member (how is the collective going to help?)

Think ahead and be ready for a worst-case scenario: What if your collective is raided? Have a plan of action ready. After the situation is assessed and you consult with your attorney, are you going to immediately re-open? In some instances, the answer might be yes. Every day that your dispensary is closed, more members are going elsewhere for medicine and they may never return. Do you have back-up product and funds available off-site? Remember that if the collective is raided, the authorities will likely visit the homes of all the directors and managers as well.

There should be specific plans of action for these and other potential scenarios that the management team should agree to. The various emergency plans would include detailed tasks and responsibilities delegated among the core team. There need to be clear, simple steps for who should be contacted and who is in charge of which actions. Periodically reviewing these plans will help reduce panic during an actual event. Non–management members might also need to be called upon in certain situations, such as when the entire management team is detained at one time. It is much better to be over-prepared than to be caught off-guard. This should also help you sleep better at night.

Bail Fund

If such unfortunate circumstances should arrive, you will want to have the option of bailing yourself (or other directors or employees) out of jail. You will have to weigh the options of paying the money and bailing out, or spending a few nights in jail and waiting for a chance to be released on your own recognizance. Bailing out means you will spend as little time in jail as possible; however, you will be out a few thousand dollars, depending on how high the bail is set. In California, the courts typically set bail at $20,000 to $100,000, so you would need to come up with $2,000 to $10,000 for a bail bondsman. Another benefit of bailing out is that you won't be required to abide by any terms of the district attorney. Often, when a person is released on his or her own recognizance, they cannot reopen or associate with the dispensary, so this can end up being a complicated decision. In the end, however, it's always better to have the option be yours, instead of depending on the mercy of the court.

Chapter 6 - The Heart of the Collective Model

The idea of the collective is often difficult to pin down. The state allows groups to "collectively" cultivate medical marijuana, but how does someone severely ill or handicapped help run a garden? The truth is, some can't, and most don't want to. Members' "contributions" will mainly be in the form of money, but the collective should allow members to contribute and volunteer in various ways. In doing this, the collective can utilize the many talents of its members. You may have members who are lawyers, doctors, or accountants, and having them provide free services will be very beneficial to the collective; Be creative, and keep in mind that the more members volunteer, the more the collective can thrive. Keep a log that records each member's volunteer activities and have them sign and date a document verifying each shift.

Until early 2012 California district attorneys were prosecuting collectives that only had a small percentage of members assisting with the growing of marijuana. Theses DA's took the narrow interpretation that all members must "come together" in "some way" to cultivate the marijuana. Seeing that this would be next to impossible for your standard collective, it makes 99% of all medical marijuana collectives invalid and puts the associated directors at risk arrest. Luckily, in February of 2012 Los Angeles' 2nd District of Appeals overruled a landmark case (The People v. Colvin). This decision rejected this notion that the California DA's were using. The original conviction of Colvin was because the collective he founded had close to 5,000 members and only a small number of growers (14 to be exact), which the California Attorney General said was insufficient. Colvin was not allowed to use the medical (marijuana) defense and was convicted of operating outside the medical marijuana guidelines. The Court of Appeal rejected the Attorney General's vague requirement that an "unspecified number of members to engage in unspecified 'united action or participation' to qualify for the protection of [state law]." The Court of Appeals decision ultimately hinged on the comparison of marijuana collectives to grocery cooperatives - they felt it was unjust to impose different requirements to the two.

We still suggest that collectives encourage members to volunteer with various activities (as it makes sense).

Expense reimbursement

This is one of the most important areas of collective operations to understand and be in control of. We must reiterate that profits are not allowed under the

California medical marijuana laws. All exchanges of money should be thoroughly documented. Ideally, a dispensary can internally (with a small management team) grow all the medicine for its patient base; however, this is unlikely, and it would most likely limit the strains available for the patients. Typical dispensaries obtain products from multiple member growers. There are no specific laws or guidelines on how this is to be done other than "collectives and cooperatives should document each member's contribution of labor, resources, or money to the enterprise. They also should track and record the source of their marijuana," per the attorney general's guidelines (**Attachment 1**, section B.4. (page 112)). You will notice the word "should" in that statement, but once again, the current legal system believes it should more accurately read "must." It is a common practice to use code names for the growers, as long as these names can accurately be translated if needed. This will protect the growers' privacy should these documents get into the wrong hands. This is a matter the board should discuss and decide on.

Determining Reimbursement for Member Growers

Since the dispensary model is based on expense reimbursements, these need to be the core of your payment method. Growers should only be reimbursed for the expenses they incurred while growing the medicine and a "reasonable compensation" (which we cover in detail in the next chapter) for their time. A model dispensary will collect and file copies of all the growers' bills. Unfortunately, this procedure can be very time consuming and require a significant storage area. To make this more practical, the grower can complete a one-page detailed expense summary that lists all the expenditures associated with a particular harvest. [See **Attachment 5** for an example] The grower will sign off on the reimbursement document, acknowledging that the amounts listed are true and correct. This document also acknowledges that the grower will keep detailed records and receipts that the dispensary can request copies of as needed (with proper notice).

The grower should keep a detailed log of the hours they are allocating to each grow. Microsoft Excel/ Open Office or similar software programs will help create an organized report and will reduce the likelihood of mathematical errors. The grower should include all direct expenses (clones, nutrients, soil, etc.) as well as allocations for electricity, rent, labor, and travel costs. Please keep in mind that compensation should be reasonable. There have been examples in the California courts where the judge accepted a grower receiving $35/hr. (which was the same rate of his previous job). The labor rate is the most flexible component of the reimbursement equation. Depending on the quality of the product, the grower should be willing to reduce their wage to make the transaction reasonable to the collective. Travel expenses and rent allocation (if the grow site is also residence) are also flexible and can be adjusted within reason to get to an amount agreeable to both the dispensary and the grower. Nothing in the law states that the dispensary is required to accept every grower's medicine or is required to reimburse the grower for specific expenses.

Compensation

This section provides details on the salaries and/or wages of individuals working at the dispensary. This is a very important topic that will be referred to time and time again. In California, individual earnings/wages are capped at a "reasonable compensation." What is a reasonable compensation? There is no straight or easy answer. However, as with all items related to medical marijuana, you should be ready to defend your answer in court. The IRS defines reasonable compensation as "the value that would ordinarily be paid for like services by like enterprises under like circumstances." There are no real standards to go by other than other (similar) non-profit businesses. It really comes down to the type of work you are doing for the collective, the hours worked and the number of members you are serving. Your education level and previous employment history should also be considered. One of the best determining factors is the pay rate of others in similar occupations in similar industries. It would be hard to defend a receptionist making $100 an hour, while that wage for a seasoned dispensary director might be acceptable. It is not uncommon for directors/CEOs of hospitals to make $250,000 to over $1M per year. In our opinion, it is unreasonable for a new collective director or founder to make a $200K salary, although it is probably not out of the question for a mature, high-volume dispensary.

Guidestar, an information service company that specializes in reporting on U.S. nonprofit companies, recommends the following guidance on salaries:

   i. The salary/rate transactions are approved by an authorized body of the organization.
   ii. The authorized body uses "appropriate data" to determine comparability prior to making a decision.
   iii. The authorized body documents the basis for its determination while making its decision.[xiv]

As the wages increase, more documentation should be kept, including any comparative salary analysis. The board of directors will make all decisions about compensation, as discussed in the Incorporating and Compliance sections earlier. The collective members should be voting on a majority of the board of directors and they should ultimately feel comfortable with the wages being paid. The members should also have access to compensation information (in the BOD minutes) if requested. When marijuana is legalized, these guidelines will disappear and the compensation ceiling will be lifted.

Consignment of Marijuana (grown by members)

Depending on the finances/cash flow of the collective, it might make sense to have the growers provide their product on consignment – meaning they provide the product and only get paid as the members purchase it from the collective. The good part about these transactions is that the collective doesn't need to put out any money up front for the product. The downside is that some experienced growers don't want to participate in this, and it also makes record-keeping more difficult. Growers can become disgruntled if they aren't paid in a timely way or if expectations aren't met, and product can be returned to the grower if it isn't purchased after a given amount of time. All these items should be considered and discussed before the medicine is taken from the grower. Please keep these items in mind, as you want the whole organization to run smoothly.

Ideally, a grower would be a member for a minimum number of days, such as 90, before they provide medicine to the dispensary. However, this is currently not required by law. This would make it literally possible that the product was grown after the patient became a member of the collective. Oftentimes, a new patient has excess marijuana they wish to share with the collective. (Please refer to the professional MMJ Language Section, in Chapter 7). The courts may argue that it would be impossible for a "collective cultivation" to take place if the marijuana is already grown. If the dispensary doesn't need to participate in this activity to survive, it is better to get medicine from a small circle of members. The dispensary should have rules in place to ensure that it isn't violating the cultivation guidelines. Make sure to stay on top of new developments in court. You will note in **Attachment 5** that all growers are vouching for the cultivation expenses claimed and stating that they personally grew the product. Before the attorney general's guidelines were released in 2008, there were people who brokered marijuana and served as the intermediaries/middlemen between the growers and the dispensaries. These brokers would buy large quantities of marijuana from growers, selling it at a premium to various dispensaries. The attorney general's guidelines basically disallow this activity. A collective should "not . . . buy marijuana from or sell to non-members," and cooperatives "should only provide a means for facilitating or coordinating transactions between members." Dispensary operators need to be aware of this activity and not condone it.

In summary, select patients/individuals (with valid doctor recommendations) are allowed to collectively cultivate marijuana for their medical needs. The more hands-on and involved every member is within the organization, the better. Unfortunately, even then you are never immune to prosecution. Make your organization as transparent as possible.

Chapter 7 - Requirements of Collective Membership

Membership Agreements

In general, the membership agreement is a contract between the medical marijuana patient and the collective or co-op. This membership agreement is the patient's commitment (and promise) that they will abide by all the requirements laid out in the bylaws of the collective. The collective must either give each new member a copy of the bylaws or have a copy on-site for review.

The state guidelines say that "the cycle should be a **closed circuit** of marijuana cultivation and consumption with no purchases or sales to or from non-members." A California district attorney recently stated that "just signing a document doesn't mean anything" and that this practice is a farce. We beg to differ. As far as we know, all that an individual is required to do in purchasing a home or taking out a loan is to sign a document. Why would this require anything different?

In a perfect world, all members of a collective would contribute the same amount of money, the same amount of time and/or labor, and the entire product produced would be equally split among all members. However, not everyone wants to dig holes and spray neem oil on plants. The average collective member doesn't know much about growing marijuana, and you wouldn't want to touch medicine they grew with a ten-foot pole. Although marijuana does survive in many conditions, it is not easy to produce quality, healthy bud. Some people want to contribute labor (in the form of growing medicine or working in the dispensary), while most members will only want to contribute money to reimburse the collective.

Please see **Attachment 6** for an example of a membership agreement.

Member Interaction and Community Involvement

Management needs to stay in close contact with the members. Keep a suggestion box available, and encourage members to leave feedback. This allows members to leave anonymous notes or suggestions for management, which is often the best way to determine what is and is not working well at the collective.

Now more than ever, collective members need to band together. Gone are the days when all you needed was to ensure that every member had a valid doctor's recommendation. It has become more complicated to provide medical marijuana to patients.

Patients should also be encouraged to volunteer for other local non-profit organizations in the name of the collective. The collective can also support events by organizing members to volunteer for various such as a beach clean-up, Earth Day or United Way's Day of Caring. This is a great way to help break down the stereotypes of medical marijuana patients and solidify the collective as a positive entity in the community. If you put in hard work, it won't go unrecognized.

Documentation:

The collective will need to keep current compliance and membership records available for officials to review. Given the nature of this business, it is better to keep a majority of the financial records off-site. Having hard-copy records on-site is a catch 22: It's damned if you do, damned if you don't. Hopefully you will never be raided by law enforcement but if you are, it's better that they seize as few financial documents as possible. It is better to be able to provide the district attorney with your records on your terms (upon the advice of your attorney, of course). This will help you avoid the records being misinterpreted, taken out of context, and possibly manipulated. Accounting records can be kept online; QuickBooks, as well as other secure online accounting software, is one option. There is also specific MMJ software for tracking the sales of your product. See the Accounting Section in Chapter 8 for more details.

Medical Records/Database

Medical records and recommendations are required to be kept on-site. You can keep physical copies or save a digital PDF copy in the computer system. Databases are available that keep these items together for easy viewing, and they can be an efficient system for the collective. MMJOS is a great program for tracking patients; see MMJOS in the endnotes for more information.

HIPAA Laws

Title II of the law protects a patient's privacy by preventing the disclosure of medical conditions by health care providers, medical billing services or insurers. Review the government's website for more information. [xv]

Other Miscellaneous Items

- You should have password protection on all your programs to decrease the likelihood of unwanted viewers.
- All city business licenses and sales permits should be easily visible at the entrance to the dispensary.
- All dispensary employee documentation should be kept on-site.

Initial Visit/Consultation with Potential Members

Membership Agreement and Bylaw Review

All patients must have a valid doctor's recommendation to become a member of the collective or enter the dispensing area of the collective. Whoever is consulting with potential members needs to be very thorough and detail oriented. In the old days, collectives could rush new patients in, give them the membership documents, and not take care to be sure they reviewed them. Now, procedures need to be in place to ensure that new patients understand the agreement they are signing. Upon his or her signature, the signor is becoming an active member of this collective organization, which requires more than just buying medicine (as we have discussed before). In addition to signing the membership agreement, they should acknowledge that they have read it (with initials on each page) and sign off on the bylaws. New members should be encouraged to attend collective meetings and vote on specific issues. Members should also understand the hierarchy of the collective and who its current board members are. The new members should be encouraged to ask questions, and you should let them know that all aspects of the business will be transparent.

Depending on the city you are operating in, patients might not be allowed to purchase product on the first visit. Also, some cities are only allowing local residents to be members of the dispensary. If this is the case, you need to modify your procedures to ensure that you are efficiently meeting these requirements.

Verifying Doctors' Recommendations

There will most likely be a few local doctors who will be providing a majority of your members with their recommendations. You will need to ensure that each patient's recommendation is valid, and check each patient's ID to verify the name and age.

Depending on each doctor's preference, you can verify the recommendations by telephone or via the Internet. Tracking the expiration dates of recommendations is extremely important, and doing so will be made easier with spreadsheets or other software programs that will even provide you with a warning a few weeks out so you can remind patients before their recommendations expire. This will give the patient time to schedule an appointment before their current recommendation expires. Remember, no one should be allowed in the dispensing area without a current recommendation. Don't make exceptions to this rule, as nothing good can come of it. You have to make it clear that it is the organization's policy and that members could potentially damage the entire collective by attempting to procure product with an expired recommendation.

Patients are required to have a current California identification card, such as a driver's license, when signing up as a member. Always make a copy of their ID to verify patients on future visits.

Also, treat every new member as if he or she were an undercover police officer. This mentality will force you to go through all the collective's procedures and ensure that you aren't leaving any loose ends that could trip you up later on.

Medical Language

To function smoothly in the medical marijuana industry, you should get used to using medical marijuana-friendly language. Here are some examples of commonly used terms:

- "Cannabis" instead of "marijuana."
- "Member growers" instead of "grower" or "vendor."
- "Patient" or "member" instead of "client" or "customer."

Although using these terms might seem insignificant, it is a good habit to get into. The use of incorrect terminology (which could signify illegal transactions) can raise the interests of law enforcement. So don't create any additional burdens for your organization; it should not only be run professionally, it should also sound professional.

Chapter 8 - Day to Day Operations

Knowing your Medical Marijuana

Anyone in charge of distributing medical marijuana to patients (AKA "bud tenders") should be familiar with the products they are providing. The best way to become familiar with the products is by sampling the various strains, as well as past experience. Be aware that identical strains can vary significantly given different growing conditions. Samples should be provided to the employees of the collective and feedback noted, and the information should be available for your patients/members. New patients will need to be provided with information regarding the various products available and their potency. The bud tender will need to make recommendations as to what products will best meet each patient's needs; there are innumerable types of marijuana that provide treatment for a great variety of medical conditions. Medical marijuana users come in all shapes and sizes, and their medical marijuana needs can be significantly different. Along with product recommendations, you should provide dosage information to novice patients. Keep in mind that various edible products should be available for those patients who can't smoke, and be sure you make the potency of those products known, as well.

Also, be aware that you will need to carefully inspect all the marijuana that is being brought into and sold at the collective for such risks as mold, mildew and pests. Unfortunately, there is dirty medicine out there, and it can come from either novice or large-scale, professional growers. A digital scope or jeweler's eyepiece with 30X magnification or greater should allow you to detect most of these problems. The Releaf Center in Denver provides a basic brochure for its patients (**Attachment 7**), which is a simple reference document containing some warning signs that all providers and patients should be aware of.

When assessing medical cannabis for quality, some of the physical characteristics you will look for include density, dryness, color, crystals, hairs and, hopefully, no seeds☺ Ideally, the bud will be fairly fluffy with heavy crystallization and have a pungent aroma. The presence of crystals (trichomes) or resin will indicate a decent level of THC. However, you will want to make sure the buds are properly dried so the weight is accurate and so mold can't incubate.

Strains

There are three distinctly different kinds of marijuana/cannabis: *Cannabis sativa*, *Cannabis indica*, and *Cannabis ruderalis*. *Cannabis ruderalis* is an uncommon variety that grows wild in parts of Eastern Europe and Russia. It's occasionally used in hybrids (the intentional crossing of two different genotypes of Cannabis) to help the resulting plants be better able to cope with harsh climates. The common *sativa* and *indica* strains possess very different characteristics.

Sativa

Sativas are tall, thin plants, with much narrower leaves and a lighter green color. The buds produced are typically loosely packed and lighter than the indica variety. Sativas grow very quickly and (in extreme cases) can reach heights of 20 feet in a single season. This strain originated in equatorial regions of the globe, including Colombia, Mexico, Thailand and Southeast Asia. Once a sativa plant begins to flower, they can take anywhere from 10 to 16 weeks to fully mature, which is much longer than the indica plant that will fully mature in 6-8 weeks. (xxviii)

The high of a sativa is described as cerebral, social and energetic. Sativa strains are most associated with laughter, long discussions about nothing, and enhanced audio and visual senses. Super Silver Haze and Headband are two examples of the sativa strain. Some patients experience a specific focus on details and can have a heightened sense of enjoyment.

Indica

Indicas originated in the hash-producing countries of the world, such as Afghanistan, Morocco, and Tibet. These are short, dense plants, with broad leaves, and they are often a darker green. Indica buds will be thick and dense, with flavors and aromas ranging from pungent skunk to sweet and fruity. The smoke from an indica is generally a body-type of high, relaxing and mellow. [xvi]

The high of an indica is described as feeling relaxed and lethargic. This cannabis is known for providing a heavy body buzz that slows a person down. This is the best type of cannabis for easing pain or to help a patient fall asleep. Two typical indica strains are OG Kush and Grand Daddy Purple.

A good indica/sativa cross can give patients the best of both worlds. Cross-breeding of plants creates hybrid strains that contain the desirable characteristics of both strains. Breeders work hard to develop strains that will give you a well-balanced head high, matched with a relaxing body high.

Active ingredients: (Cannabinoids)

There are over 80 identified cannabinoids in the cannabis plant, and each strain has its own unique genetic combination.

The active cannabinoids each have unique physiological effects, and many combinations actually appear to have synergistic and antagonistic effects.

The following are the most common natural herbal cannabinoids found in cannabis:

Delta-9-tetrahydrocannabinol (THC):

Euphoric, stimulant, muscle relaxant, anti-epileptic, anti-emetic, anti-inflammatory, appetite stimulating, bronchio-dilating, hypotensive, anti-depressant and analgesic effects.

Cannabidiol (CBD):

Lessens the psychoactive effects of THC and has sedative and analgesic effects.

Cannabichromene (CBC):

Promotes the effects of THC and has sedative and analgesic effects.

Cannabigerol (CBG):

Has sedative effects and anti-microbial properties as well as lowering intra-ocular pressure. CBG is the biogenetic precursor of all other cannabinoids.

Cannabinol (CBN):

A mildly psychoactive degradation of THC, its primary effects are as an anti-epileptic, and to lower intra-ocular pressure. Every strain of cannabis will have varying amounts of these various cannabinoids.

Pricing the Medicine

A collective is not for profit and is in place to provide qualified patients with marijuana for medical needs. <u>Ultimately, the collective should not have a profit at year end</u>. If surplus cash/income is left over, it is up to the members to decide how best to utilize this. A few possibilities are to make capital purchases/improvements (e.g., buy a van for collective operations and to transport members; provide members with cash back or free product; or donate the money to charity.

The collective should aim to charge (per transaction) an amount to cover the cost to produce the product and an allocation towards overhead expenses. There are various ways to do this, but the best way is to estimate the monthly sales and monthly overhead expenses and add a percentage on top of the product costs (for each sale) for overhead expenses. In doing this, each sale will contribute toward the operating expenses of the collective. Please keep in mind that there are other ways to calculate, but the end result should be the same: Get the members their medicine at the best price possible.

Examples:

Assumptions (for the following two examples):

1. The Collective estimates selling about 2 ounces a day for the month, open 6 days a week (24 days x 2 ounces) = 3 pounds per month
    i. Average reimbursement (cost) to the collective of a pound of medicine is $3,500. So we estimate the total monthly cost of the collective's medicine to be $10,500 (or 3 pounds x $3,500)

2. Estimated monthly operating expenses of the collective are $8,000 (payroll, rent, utilities, etc).

3. Given these assumptions, our expenses are roughly 76% of the cost of our product ($8,000/$10,500 = 0.762). So if our estimates were right on, we would sell 3 pounds for $10,500 x 1.76 = $18,480, which would cover our product and expenses (less $20 lost to rounding).

4. 1 pound converts to 453.59 grams, rounded to 450 grams per pound.

<u>Example 1:</u> Determining the selling price of a specific strain:

A member grows 1 pound sour diesel, with all expenses to grow, including labor at a reasonable rate per hour, of $3,000. The price per gram would be roughly $6.67 ($3,000/450). This is our base price. Now we add our overhead costs estimated at 76% of the product cost (per iii. above), so our basic price per gram to charge members would be $11.74 ($6.67 x 1.76)

<u>Example 2:</u> Determining the selling price of a specific strain (same assumptions as Example 1):

A member grows 1 pound OG Kush, with all expenses to grow, including labor at a reasonable rate per hour, of $4,000. The price per gram would be roughly $8.89 ($4,000/450). This is our base price. Now we add our overhead costs estimated at 76% of the product cost, so our basic price per gram to charge members would be $15.64 ($8.89 x 1.76)

Your equations will need to be adjusted at least monthly as your estimates will change based on actual results (and new forecasts). Keep in mind you can add a cushion into your overhead percentage for any emergency funds or other items the collective feels are appropriate.

In most industries, consumers are given a discount for buying in bulk. Law enforcement has argued that this shows that the operations are "really" operating for profit; however, we would argue that if a member buys in bulk, he or she should pay less overhead, as they will visit the collective fewer times per month, thus using fewer resources. You can add these assumptions into your calculations.

<u>Example #3</u>: Reduced pricing for larger purchases

- $1/8^{th}$ ounce is 3.5 grams with a 10% reduction in overhead allowance
- 66% instead of 76% = $14.76/gram (8.89 x 1.66)
- $1/8^{th}$ price = $51.65 ($14.76 x 3.5 gram)

Make sure you document all your assumptions and monitor your finances often to make sure the collective isn't over- or under-charging the members.

Sales Tax

You can either add sales tax on top of the sales price or include it in the price to keep the numbers rounded.

<u>Option a</u>: $15.64 gram with 8% sales tax ($1.25) added would be $16.89 total.

<u>Option b</u>: Charge $17 which is the $15.64 gram price and $1.25 tax rounded to the nearest dollar. This would keep your cash and change transactions simpler but will complicate your internal accounting.

<u>Option b(2)</u>: Determine the final price (with tax) that you wish to charge and work backwards to find the sales amount before tax.

Equation: Final price = x + (sales tax*x)
20 = x + (.08x),
20/1.08x
X = $18.51

Metric to American-Standard Weight Conversion

3.5 grams = 1/8 ounce
7 grams = 1/4 ounce
14 grams = 1/2 ounce
28 grams = 1 ounce
454 grams = 1 pound
All ratios have been rounded.

Inventory Controls

Medical marijuana is a very valuable and sought-after product. You will need solid procedures in place to guarantee that the dispensary's medicine is not being misappropriated (stolen). This will require frequent physical counts of the inventory, as well as accurate accounting of sales. We have attached a spreadsheet that you can use as a reference or template. Ideally, your point-of-sale system (POS) will track inventory, and you will need to know what the current inventory is at any given time. A variance report (inventory system vs. actual) will need to be created. If your greenroom and sales register employee switch shifts mid-day, you will want to cross-check by performing a count then as well. You might encounter an instance where one strain is a few grams short but another strain is a few grams over, but that would most likely indicate that the wrong product was run through the computer system.

You need to be more concerned with the overall variance. The variance report is a great control to have in place and should deter employees from trying to misappropriate product, and you will definitely want to make sure your POS can only be adjusted by a manager. Also, any adjustment or product removed from the system should be recorded and kept on file. If your employees are changing each day, a recount should be done in the morning to verify the existing inventory. This makes every worker accountable for their sales and inventory counts. Management should constantly be looking for holes in the system and correcting any that are found.

Depending on the quality of your medicine, a certain percentage will turn to shake. This should be kept in a daily shake jar and added to the totals to reconcile for the day. This shouldn't create a problem in general, but please be aware that there is a potential for small misappropriations of "good" product that are then substituted for by old shake.

If you don't have a POS system in place, you can create the same procedure manually. You will need to track and add all your daily activity. Create a "tally sheet" with the various strains that can be quickly marked off each time a sales takes place. At the end of the day, total the sales per strain and remove that amount from your beginning inventory. See **Attachment 8** for examples. At the end of each day, your calculated inventory should tie to your actual inventory. Microsoft Excel or Open Office software will make the accounting much easier.

If your volume picks up, you may want to streamline your inventory process by having pre-weighed packages (e.g., 2 ounces total, pre-weighed into one 1/4 ounce, eight 1/8ths, and 21 grams) that you can move from the safe to the floor easily. You will typically want to have smaller quantities to work with in the green room. You don't want to be picking grams out of your larger (¼ pound +) bags, which will deteriorate the product over time. If someone wants a larger quantity, you can take that directly from the safe without affecting the green room inventory. This format will also make the daily inventory counting simpler.

Another way to simplify things is to use the same units, such as only pounds or 2 oz. bags in the safe, and anything less in the green room. You should keep a separate listing of the safe inventory and that should be updated when products are moved.

Receipts:

Retain a copy of the receipts from each day's sales. If you have a computer-based point of sales system, saving an external backup is sufficient. If you are using carbon-copy paper receipts, staple daily sales together and take them to storage. You will need to retain these for a minimum of three years, and they will be needed if you are subject to a financial audit. To be cautious, it is probably best to keep the bulk of your receipts and financial records at a secure location off-site.

Bank accounts:

It is easier to run a business with a bank account, and many service providers (e.g., payroll) require that you have one. A bank account will also give the dispensary the convenience and flexibility of using checks and electronic transfers. Checks provide a much better trail than cash and money orders. Currently, most banks won't accept dispensary customers. However, it is still worth the effort to try to open an account. Smaller, local banks and credit unions are probably your best bet. It will help if you already have a relationship with the bank or a banker. If you can't do without a bank account, you might need to expand the services offered and amend the collective's bylaws.

In order to open a business bank account you will need the following: a business tax ID (EIN), Articles of Incorporation, a current statement of information, and possibly a corporate resolution defining bank signers. At least two of three officers of the corporation must be present as well.

Worst case scenario: As part of your overall procedures, it isn't recommended that you keep a high cash reserve in your bank account because, unfortunately, the police or the government can seize your funds with the snap of their fingers. So it's best to keep cash reserves in a secure site away from the dispensary, such as the property of a member of the board of directors, or other agreed-upon location. As expenses are due, you can make adequate deposits to cover them. To reiterate, we are not condoning any illegal activities or money laundering—you should have accurate records regardless of how funds are received or stored. Your goal is to protect the collective's assets. It is better to play it safe than to risk having your funds seized, and hope to get them back after a successful trial.

Free medicine

California medical marijuana should be available to all people regardless of their income level. Unfortunately, the current Medicare system does not help patients obtain it. The collective should have a policy in place (approved by the board) where it will provide medicine (or discounts) to needy individuals who can't afford it. There are many ways to go about doing this, such as further discounting your lower-end medicine, which will be helpful to some patients. If too many patients are claiming hardships, you can create a lottery system and pick a given number of patients to help per week. Don't forget to be compassionate and help those in need, and remember to closely track all of the medicine that is given away. This should be incorporated into the collective's inventory control system (discussed in Chapter 8).

Accounting

Accounting is a huge part of any business, but it is extremely important to a dispensary; dispensaries deal with a lot of cash and they are under more scrutiny (from various organizations) than other businesses. You need to weigh the pros and cons of using an outside bookkeeper/accounting firm or doing it yourself (internally).

If no one in your organization has a business background, at a minimum you will need to have someone set up your accounting system and give you instructions. You won't be able to get good information out of a bad system. You need to assess the skills of your employees and the time available for them to do your accounting work; you need someone who is competent enough to make accurate entries and keep clean records. You will also want to have systems in place when the collective gets busy. It is much easier and more useful to keep your records current, instead of having to go back months later and making data entries.

A good bookkeeper or consultant should be able to set up some accounting procedures and give you (and other employees who will be keeping records) a basic understanding of accounting. This will get your organization on the right track. The consultant should also provide you with periodic check-ups to ensure that things are running smoothly. You can create an "unknown"/misc. account within your accounting program for entries you have questions about.

Establishing dispensary procedures will ensure that all income and expense items are recorded every day. You will also need a procedure for collecting receipts and recording any cash payouts. Typically, you would write this information down in a ledger and file the receipts, and at the end of the day you would reconcile your income and expenses and record everything in your accounting software. Reconciling needs to be done each night to ensure that there are no unexplained discrepancies in either cash or inventory (as outlined in the Inventory control section). Ideally, entries would be made every day into the accounting system, but weekly is acceptable; just be sure you don't get too far behind. Keep in mind that the further behind you get, the harder it is to remember or track down additional information, if needed.

The accounting software will allow you to run periodic profit and loss statements, known as P&L, which you can use to assess the efficiency of the business and compare to the budget (as we recommended in the Budget section, Chapter 5). This will keep management in alignment with the business and can allow for more frequent and accurate product price adjustments. These financial records will also make it easier for your tax accountant to complete the necessary filings.

Chances are that your dispensary will receive product on consignment (review the Consignment Section, in Chapter 6). The dispensary will owe these growers money once their products are sold. You will need to track these debts, and it is probably best to do this within the accounting software, although you can keep a separate spreadsheet for this if you find that easier. These expenses need to be included in your accounting system at some point for your P&L to be accurate. Keep in mind that your overall COGS will be incorrect until all the consignment product is sold through.

There are a few point-of-sale software programs that have been designed specifically for dispensaries. Unfortunately, we haven't seen one that seamlessly interacts with a patient database system and a robust accounting program. Typically, if you are looking for top-of-the-line programs, you will need separate systems for storing patient data, sales and inventory software, and an accounting program.

Many traditional businesses are moving to paperless offices, where all items are scanned in and the paper copy is shredded or recycled. This paperless procedure might be very advantageous to dispensaries that want to keep a tight control on who gets access to financial data.

There are also bookkeepers who are available to work remotely: You fax or email your daily ledger and receipts, and they will do all the inputs for you. The dispensary should produce monthly, if not weekly, profit and loss reports.

Merchant services

In order to accept credit card payments, you will need a merchant account that typically links to your bank account. These are a good option to have for your patients, and it will often increase patient purchases. However, the merchant service business is highly competitive; beware of hidden fees, high percentage rates, and cancellation fees. As of July 1, 2012, U.S. banks will no longer be able to process credit card transactions for medical marijuana dispensaries. However, there are alternatives available. We are familiar with The Transaction Group, which offers a modified debit/credit card swipe that charges a fixed fee per transaction. The setup fees vary, and there is a $2.00 per transaction charge that can be paid by the collective or the patient. The good news is that the new system typically ends up costing less than a traditional merchant account. Please visit their website (listed in our Resources section) for more details.

Another potential provider worth looking into is PayPal Here which accepts credit card payment through smart phones. This option will likely only qualify if the collective offers a significant portion of non-marijuana products or services.

Advertising/Marketing (Finding new Collective members)

It is very important to know both your city and law enforcement views on medical marijuana advertisements. Please research your local market and keep in mind that law enforcement will be reading your ads. Avoid placing or responding to personal ads about medical marijuana, as these have commonly been used to trap people.

Referrals and Word of Mouth

Depending on your situation and location, you most likely already know a handful of people who would like to collectively grow with you. The best way to round up interested parties is word of mouth. The smaller, more tightly knit collectives seem to avoid problems. Providing high-quality medicine is the best way to gain word-of-mouth referrals. Keep a friendly, clean, professional environment that you are proud of.

Talk with members of other collectives to see what they like and don't like about their own organizations. Put your heart into your organization and do your best to make the members happy. Medical marijuana patients often have friends and associates who are also patients, and using that network is one of the best ways to add to your membership base. Incentive medicine or discounts for referrals can be a good motivation for existing patients to help recruit new patients for you. Concurrently, offering first-time specials to members will increase the likelihood of getting new members. A broader patient base will allow for better, cheaper medicine, and everyone should be excited about that. However, please be aware that these activities can appear to be more in line with a for-profit retail business rather than a nonprofit medical collective, and you may want to avoid them. In a perfect world you wouldn't need to advertise for memberships. Please observe your specific environment and consult with your attorney before embarking on a marketing program.

Referring Doctors

This should be a very powerful source for generating members. Make sure you visit all the local doctors who are supplying patients with marijuana recommendations and make them aware of your collective, because the doctors have first access to potential members. Doctors will typically provide patients with a list of local collectives, so you want to make sure yours is on that list! Doctors have regulations against referring people (with bias) to specific collectives or having a financial interest (via kickbacks). You just want to ensure equal treatment and make sure your organization is known. You will also be contacting these offices to verify patients, so in any case you want to strive for a good relationship.

Print Ads

Many collectives are choosing to advertise in local papers. All written advertising should be professional and advertise to medicinal patients only. Reference "Full Compliance with Prop 215 and SB 420." Also, include any local laws/ordinances that might be applicable.

And remember, business cards are cheap, easy to carry and effective.

Web advertising

WeedTracker

This is a website for medical marijuana dispensaries, and they charge an annual fee to list a collective. There was a time when it was almost mandatory that you have a listing on this website. This site has a number of dispensaries listed and it is a good way to get anonymous customer comments; this is the dispensary-specific version of Yelp.com. Use this as a learning tool, but don't become obsessed with bad reviews, as it isn't uncommon for other dispensaries to try to discredit others. For that reason, it is worth trying to have negative comments removed if you feel they are unfair or unwarranted. Stay in contact with the site's administrator, and try to stay in good standing with them. They will ultimately decide what comments to allow or remove.

Pot Locator

This is a free website where you can list your medical marijuana collective. They allow you to post pictures of your collective as well. They offer advanced features and enhanced listings for a fee.

There are many ways to increase your web presence for free, such as Yellow Pages sites that allow you to add your web page, detailed information and photos. Google also has a "Places" application where you can add information about your organization. This information is then available through smart phones and other media devices.

Also, try Universal Business Listing (UBL), a local search industry service dedicated to acting as a central collection and distribution point for business information online. This will quickly enhance your web presence and save you time, as it will distribute your information to multiple search engines and websites. www.ubl.org

Social Media: Facebook and Twitter

It's funny to have to write about Facebook in a MMJ guide, but this type of social media is still on the cutting edge of marketing. This is particularly true for an entity like a collective. What better way to find like-minded people in your area, and the price is right (it's free). This can be a tremendously useful source, for not only cultivating new members, but also for providing updates to existing ones. Not everyone uses Facebook, but those who do use it use it often, so it is a good way to stay in constant contact with members. If the dispensary is having a slow day, what do you have to lose by sending out an immediate special invite to members? You have nothing to lose—it's free and it's fast. Someone in your organization should be put in charge of making updates to the account every couple of days, if not daily.

Sponsorships

Help local organizations or events while gaining exposure. Donating money or services is a great way to kill two birds with one stone; by sponsoring a local charity event, you gain needed exposure while helping out your community. This is a subtle way to get your name out, and it identifies you as a compassionate organization. Remember (as mentioned in the Pricing section earlier in this chapter), ultimately any cash donations should be approved by the board of directors and/or members per the collective's bylaws.

Taxes

Federal and State Income taxes

To reiterate, a collective should not be making a profit. It is expected that the corporation will show a loss for the year. If the corporation has a profit, these funds should be distributed back to the members and management should make adjustments going forward to zero out the profit. This can be done through lowering the price charged for the medicine, adding new services for the members, making improvements to the collective, increasing in wages, or a combination of those. The board will need to approve these changes and they should be documented in the collective's minutes.

Federal Taxes

- Form 1120 - U.S. Corporation Income Tax Return
- Due each year by 15th day of third month of operations (typically March 15 or September 15th with an extension, for corporations with a calendar year end)

California Taxes

- Form 100 - California Corporation Income Tax Return
- Same due dates as federal return

- o   Due each year by 15th day of third month of operations
- Subject to $800/year franchise tax fee

It must be noted what could happen to a collective in a worst-case scenario:

The IRS requires that you report "all income from whatever source derived." This can include illegal activities (i.e. gambling, prostitution, and drug sales). IRS code § 280E discusses "Expenditures in connection with the illegal sale of drugs," which is where they classify medical marijuana. The code reads as follows: "No deduction or credit shall be allowed for any amount paid or incurred during the taxable year in carrying on any trade or business if such trade or business (or the activities which comprise such trade or business) consists of trafficking in controlled substances (within the meaning of schedule I and II of the Controlled Substances Act) which is prohibited by Federal law or the law of any State in which such trade or business is conducted."[xvii]

Section 280E of the Tax Code (above) was originally designed to affect large-scale illegal drug traffickers and provided the feds with a financial weapon in the war against drugs. This code is now being used to close down medical marijuana dispensaries. In 2011, the Harborside Health Center (in San Francisco) was sent a bill for $2.4 million dollars for back taxes relating to its marijuana sales; the IRS basically disallowed all the cost of doing business. Although it sounds counter-intuitive, the IRS will allow the entity to deduct the cost of the marijuana (COGS), but nothing else. So the payroll, rent, and other normal business expenses don't count. This situation is still being appealed.

However, in CHAMP v. Commissioner of the Internal Revenue Service, 128 T.C. No. 14(2007), a ground-breaking, national impact case, the defense challenged the IRS's position that dispensaries could not take any ordinary business deductions. The win in this case allowed the marijuana dispensaries to deduct most of their expenses that were needed to operate their care-giving facilities. Please note that this cooperative offered many non-marijuana services to severely ill patients.

It is for this reason that you will want to incorporate other products and services into your dispensary. This way, you will be protecting yourself for a worst-case scenario. The IRS will allow deductions for general expenses associated with the non-marijuana services. Read U.S. Tax Court case "CALIFORNIANS HELPING TO ALLEVIATE MEDICAL PROBLEMS, INC., Petitioner v. COMMISSIONER OF INTERNAL REVENUE, Respondent" for more details. [xviii]

Sales taxes

Sales taxes are paid through the California Board of Equalization (BOE).

You must submit a form BOE 400 SPA (seller permit application) or take it into the nearest field office. You should be able to receive a seller's permit on the same day if you go in person.

You can choose to not state the products being sold on the application. "The Board will issue a seller's permit to an applicant who does not indicate the products being sold. The applicant, however, will be asked to sign a waiver acknowledging that his or her application is incomplete, which may result in the applicant not being provided with complete information regarding obligations as a holder of a seller's permit, or notified of future requirements by the Board related to the products sold. Applicants who do not wish to indicate the type of products they are selling should leave the line, "What items do you sell?" blank and discuss the issue with a Board representative." An alternative would be creative and use broader terms, such as natural/holistic medicine or wellness products.

Your sales tax should be collected on all retail sales at the dispensary (this would typically include everything, unless you receive money for services). The percentage of sales will vary city to city as various cities and counties can add various taxes. See the BOE website for the exact amount of tax required in your city. http://www.boe.ca.gov/cgi-bin/rates.cgi

Sales tax returns are typically filed quarterly (even when prepayments are required). If sales will average above $17,000 a month, prepayment of sales taxes will be due monthly. (RTC section 6471) See CPPM 510.025 for due dates.

The easiest way to file your return is to sign up and use the BOE's e-filing services. You will receive an express login code that will allow you to simply enter your sales figures and submit online. For more information, visit the BOE website at http://www.boe.ca.gov/

In June 2007, the California BOE issued "Information on Sales Tax and Registration for Medical Marijuana Sellers." The BOE's policy was modified in 2005 to allow for sellers of medical marijuana to obtain a permit. Previously, the Board would not issue a seller's permit when sales consisted only of medical marijuana. Please review **Attachment 9** for more information.

1099s

A Form 1099 should be issued to everyone, (other than corporations, which you don't need to worry about) that the collective paid $600 or more to during a calendar year. This would include your landlord and member growers and any other contractors that were paid more than $600.

The corporation exclusion does not apply to attorneys and healthcare providers, so you must still issue a Form 1099 to your attorney and medical doctor even if they are incorporated. You should also issue a Form 1099 to LLCs and people operating under a DBA that you paid $600 or more to during a calendar year.

Collectives/corporations are required to have a completed Form W-9 from every payee that you are required to issue a Form 1099 to.

To avoid having to track down payees at year's end, ask every payee to complete a Form W-9 before you pay them. W-9s can be found on the IRS website www.irs.gov. 1099s are carbon copy forms that need to be requested online or picked up at a local IRS office.

Form 1099s should have been issued to recipients by January 31, 20XX and filed with the IRS within a month (by February 28, 20XX).

Chapter 9 - Other Items

Hiring Employees

Who should you hire: your friends, marijuana *connoisseur*, students? There isn't an easy answer. Your budget is going to determine how hard you have to work to find good employees. You can't expect to get a Ph.D. to work behind the counter for minimum wage. The two most important qualities for an employee are honesty and reliability. This industry deals with a lot of cash and valuable medicine. The collective needs to be able to trust all members of the operating team. Of course, you also want to have internal controls in place to safeguard the money and inventory, but you don't want to have to police the employees.

Interview all prospective employees. Have a list of questions ahead of time that you can ask during the interview. Rate the answers and write notes about each individual. You may need to do a second round of interviews if you don't get a standout the first time.

Friends can be difficult to work with, as it is hard to separate your personal life and your profession. There are two theories here: You enjoy being around your friends, and working with them will make running the collective more enjoyable; and working with your friends will put stress and strain on your friendship. The potential conflicts are specific to the structure of the management team and employees. Just keep in mind that unless you have a strong (leadership) personality, it is going to be difficult to manage a friend. This may ultimately threaten your friendship.

Make sure all employees have their medical marijuana recommendation and become members before they begin to work at the collective. We do not suggest that the collective pay for an employee's first recommendation because, theoretically, only patients can become employees. It doesn't look good if someone obtains their first recommendation as a requirement to be an employee. Also, you don't want employees testifying that they just wanted a job and you sent them to get a recommendation. However, it should be sufficient if a patient has recently obtained a recommendation. Although it shouldn't be a huge issue, you might need to make it clear that only MMJ patients will be considered.

All employees should be members of the collective. You should keep copies of the employee's medical recommendation, membership agreement, I-9 (Employee Identification Form) [xix] which should be retained and held for 3 years, and W-4 (Employee Withholding Allowance) issued by the IRS, all of which should be filed together in the employee's file. The medical recommendation and W-4 form should be updated each year.

Payroll (and associated taxes)

It is possible to do the payroll yourself using accounting software (like QuickBooks); however, payroll is a difficult, time-consuming process and is best left to the professionals. We strongly suggest you use a payroll service, such as Paychex or ADP. These payroll service companies can handle your quarterly state and federal filing requirements, but it is still good to have an understanding of these.

Workers Compensation is also required for all employees in California. This can be expensive for a collective, especially if an employee is classified as a security guard. It will be more affordable if your employees are classified as administrative or office workers. A properly set up collective shouldn't require active security guards, anyway. On average, Workers Compensation insurance will cost between 3-4% of the employee's annual wages. Unfortunately, this money is due at the beginning of the year, based on estimates. The actual fees are then adjusted at the end of the year. You can obtain this insurance through the same provider as your property insurance or through an affiliate of (or recommendation from) your payroll processor.

Division of Labor Standards Enforcement

"In California, all employers must meet workplace posting obligations. Workplace postings are usually available at no cost from the requiring agency. The Department of Industrial Relations requires employers to post information related to wages, hours and working conditions in an area frequented by employees where it may be easily read during the workday. Additional posting requirements apply to some workplaces. For a list of available safety and health postings, visit the **Cal/OSHA publications page**." [xx] Although this information is available for free on the website, you will be able to find a lot of companies selling laminated, consolidated versions for $20-$50, which you may want to consider for the aesthetics of the dispensary. A majority of small businesses in California seem to be lax about posting or updating these notices. However, being a medical marijuana dispensary will put more attention on you, and you want to be as compliant as possible. Don't give any government agencies a reason to focus on your organization.

Insurance

Property Insurance

Landlords typically require tenants to purchase property insurance as part of the lease agreement. This should not be very difficult and should cost an average of $500-$1,200 a year. This insurance protects the real estate/property in case of most disasters and can cover some of the real property inside the location as well.

Workers Compensation

Be aware that the descriptions of employees will have a great impact on the cost of coverage; it is much cheaper to categorize someone as administrative rather than security. Be aware of the differences: If someone can be classified as either administrative or a secretary, that's a better choice than security guard. However, there are now agents who specialize in dispensaries, and they can likely provide you with the best advice regarding this issue.

Other

Dispensaries now have the option of insuring their inventory, and growers can insure their harvests. This is a relatively new service that is worth looking into. Unfortunately, at this point the insurance covers only fire, theft, and robbery (not raids). Scott Sherwood at Breeze Insurance Services (http://scottsherwoodins.com) specializes in the medical marijuana industry and he should be able to help you with any of your insurance needs. Quotes are available online from various providers.

Supplies

Keeping costs down is important in every business. You want to find a balance between ordering your packaging material in bulk and not depleting your cash flow. You want to keep your price per unit as low as possible without creating money issues or taking up too much space. You should refer back to your budget on a monthly basis and see how your actual expenses matched your estimates. Try to find areas where expenses can be cut back, and also try to stay on top of your finances before you run into problems. Don't be afraid to contemplate new ideas, and research the prices of various vendors periodically to ensure that you are getting the best pricing and quality your money can buy.

Here are two suppliers that offer a variety of packaging options for your medicine:

a. www.sunpacksupply.com
b. www.caplugs.com

Cleaning

You should rotate cleaning duties among the employees, unless someone has a desire to own this activity. Your goal should be keeping the collective clean and tidy; anything less is unprofessional. Create a schedule for cleaning; it's better to do a little each day than a lot every once in a while.

Edibles

The issue of edibles is somewhat complicated. Some dispensaries have chosen not to offer them, as it raises issues with the FDA and food safety. Many patients cannot smoke their medicine due to health problems and need an alternative method of medicating. Other patients just prefer to consume medicine for the associated body high or to avoid the carcinogens associated with smoking. Some edible options should be made available, but quality control and food laws must be strictly followed.

If possible, list the amount of marijuana used to produce each edible item. It is common for patients to over-medicate on edibles because the effects of eating marijuana take at least an hour to notice, and patients are often unsure of the proper dosage and so consume too much.

Some dispensaries make their own edible products, while others have the patients or vendor make the edibles. As with all other items, please be sure you have a trustworthy source. All the products that are used for resale should be produced in a commercial kitchen. All FDA and local food laws should be followed and items properly packaged. Ensure that all edibles are clearly marked as "For Medical Use Only; keep away from children/animals, not for anyone under age 18 and compliant with SB 420/Prop 215."

Americans for Safe Access gives the following advice regarding edibles: "Problematic interactions with law enforcement may not be avoidable, but (there are) things to do to lessen that likelihood, (which) include ensuring all edibles are well wrapped and clearly labeled "for medical use." If you produce edibles yourself, ensure that: a) the ingredients and finished product are out of reach of children and people who are neither patients nor caregivers; b) the facility and tools used to produce the edibles are clean and sanitary (consider compliance with local and/or state clean room requirements); and c) the packaging of edibles does not violate copyright laws nor unduly attract the attention of youth."[xxi]

Chapter 10 - Collectively Growing Medical Marijuana

Once you have your medical recommendation, you are ready to start growing for yourself. Your doctor's recommendation should tell you how many plants you can cultivate. If you desire to grow more than your personal allowance, you will need to associate with other patients or join a local collective and let them know that you want to cultivate. Make sure you have proper documentation, including a collective cultivation agreement and patient recommendations for the number of plants you are growing. It's always better to be over-documented and grow less than your maximum allowance. Keep a copy of your documentation in plain view at the grow site with a duplicate copy off-site. Please refer back to the **Expense Reimbursement** section in **chapter 6** for information regarding compensation.

Plant Counts

The basic rule in California (based on SB420) is that a patient can possess 6 adult marijuana plants or 12 immature plants (or 8 ounces of dried marijuana) for personal use. However, these SB 420 limitations are no longer bound by state law. In 2006, the California Courts convicted an MMJ patient, Patrick Kelly, of possessing more than his maximum amount of marijuana allowed under SB 420. That case was appealed, and in January 2010 California's Second Appellate District Court overturned Kelly's conviction on the grounds that legislatively imposed limits on possession and cultivation of medical marijuana are an unconstitutional restriction to a voter-approved initiative. The appeals court believed that the original Compassionate Use Act, passed by California voters in 1996, set no limits on how much marijuana patients could possess or grow, stating only that it be for personal use.

Many doctors and law enforcement officials still use the SB 420 quantity as a guideline. Doctors can write recommendations for higher plant counts based on an individual's consumption level and medicating method. Some doctors issue recommendations for up to 99 plants or unlimited plants in a 10X10' area. Please be prepared to defend the number of plants you possess that are either reasonably related to meeting your current medical needs or related to your collective/cooperative involvement.

Calculate your allowable plant counts and have the required recommendations and cultivation agreements at the grow site. Always consider the pros and cons of a large plant count at a given location; in most cases, it is better to have a number of smaller grows than one large one. This will reduce your risk of robbery, seizure, and pest infestation ruining your entire crop.

Federal Minimum Sentences

Before 2008 (under the Bush Administration) federal law had mandatory minimum sentences for growing over a certain number of plants and other quantity-related thresholds. At that time, it was safer to keep the count below 100 plants, because going above left you open to a potential five-year prison term. Luckily for medical marijuana growers, these minimums are no longer mandatory; in 2009, Charles Lynch was convicted of federal marijuana-related charges and subject to a five-year minimum sentence. Fortunately, the judge took the specifics of the case into account and reduced his sentence to one year. As of the writing of this book, Mr. Lynch's case is back in appeals and he still hasn't served any jail time since his original arrest.

Documentation Required

Keep a draft of the corporate bylaws and grower agreements at all grow operations. Keep enough recommendations on-site to cover the total plant count. Inform the members (whose recommendations should be on-site) in case they are questioned by authorities.

Patient Growers Agreements

This is an agreement between the collective and the member grower. It should provide details of the arrangement and include the number of plants being grown (number of patients allocated to the grow with their recommendations included); the policy regarding retention of records; the expense reimbursement calculation/determination; any product restrictions (e.g., required organic grow methods); and other health concerns. The collective has rights to inspect the grow site; the grower will abide by all applicable state laws, disclaimer for liability, and any other items the board feels is appropriate. This agreement should also state that all of the medicine grown there is for the sole use of the collective and any diversion is strictly prohibited. Please visit our website for a sample of a Member-Grower Agreement (the password is "Prop215").

Quality Control

Growers can have their crops tested at laboratories (such as Cal Canna Labs) for potency, bacteria/mold activity, or pesticides. Cal Canna Labs is one of the highest-quality testing facilities. They can verify the presence of trace amounts of chemical pesticides in dried flowers and other medical cannabis concentrates. [xxii]

Growers can also have their operations certified as organic. CleanGreen, based in Crescent City, CA, will certify gardens as organic. This process starts with questions about the source of the water used, the source of electricity, how a farmer is protecting against soil erosion, the border areas (are they natural vegetation allowing for beneficial insects, or are the plants next to a toxic area, etc.), how the grower combats pests, weeds and diseases, and so on. Once the application is completed, an on-site crop inspection is scheduled. During the inspection it is confirmed that the methods the grower stated in the application are in fact the methods being used on-site. There is a thorough review of all of the inputs the grower is using: fertilizers, pest control sprays, potting soils, etc. The Clean Green Certified Program allows the same inputs that are allowed under the USDA Organic Program. They use the same input review standards as the USDA Organic Program in determining what can and cannot be used as a growing input. [xxiii]

Silence is Golden

If growing medical marijuana is something you are passionate about, you will be tempted to tell people about it; it's simply human nature. However, nothing good can come from bragging about your grow, so tell as few people as possible. This will reduce the chances that your medicine will be stolen or wrongfully raided.

Be conscious of the odor being emitted from your grow area. If you are growing indoors, you want to use air filters and fans to divert the distinct smell of the marijuana. Also be diligent about what you throw away in the garbage. It is better to dispose of grow-related materials (nutrient containers, leaf trimmings, stems, etc.) at an alternative site to reduce the chances of neighbors (or random passers-by) discovering your grow.

Starting an Indoor Grow

Planning

Create plans for your space. It saves time to plan ahead and create the room(s) that will be most efficient for you. Talk with a mentor or local hydroponics store to determine the best placement of your lights, air conditioner, fans, etc. You can discover some helpful information online if you are willing to spend some time researching. A detailed marijuana grow book will also be helpful. Don't be fooled, however: Growing quality medicine is not easy. If you are new to it, be prepared to produce sub-quality product for your first few cycles. As with any skill, practice, research, and experimentation will be required.

It is better to build your grow room right the first time, rather than trying to get up and running as quickly as possible. You will likely need to make structural changes to the location, including adding or removing walls, cutting holes for an air conditioner, intake or exhaust, and adding electricity, drains and plumbing.

Determine the number of lights and wattage per bulb you intend to use. You will need to consult with an electrician to determine the amount of energy you have available. If you are planning on needing more than a couple of 1000-watt lights, you may need to consider having a separate electrical panel installed and running 220 volts (such as those used for large appliances like washing machines) instead of the standard 110 volts that standard appliances use. Using 220 volts will provide you with the capacity to do more work but won't necessarily save you a significant amount of money. A 220 volt system also uses bigger wires that can handle more amperage. Utility companies charge you for wattage (kilowatt-hour) not amperage. A kilowatt-hour is 1000 watts of usage for one hour, approximately equal to a 1000-watt light running for one hour. Another item to consider is the length of the wires and extension cords needed from the breaker box to the ballast - the farther away, the more resistance, which causes a voltage drop (and energy loss) which could be diverted using 220 volts.

The basic electrical formula is: **Wattage / Voltage = Amperage**

An important consideration is safety: Is your electricity up to code? Avoid fire hazards and keep fire extinguishers on-site. Be prepared.

Expenses

Keep detailed records of the expenses associated with your grow. Your direct expenses would include items directly needed to grow (i.e. clones, soil, nutrients, etc.) You should also record the miles driven (that relate to the grow), allocation of rent (if using a residential property), and possibly some allocation of Internet and cell phone charges (if applicable). Create a log or record book to record the hours you worked on the grow, and update this log as often as possible. This will be a very valuable tool for calculating your reasonable compensation per hour (please refer to Chapter 6 regarding Compensation for more details). Growers are only allowed reimbursement of expenses and a reasonable compensation (which is consistent with the other collective employees or management).

Keep your expenses organized and accurate. Pick up folders and a file box from an office supply store; it is much better to develop good habits from the start, instead of working hard at the end. The typical turn-around time per cycle is 8-12 weeks of bloom time depending on the particular strain you are growing. Your expenses are likely to include the following:

Start Up costs
- Structural changes (wood, drywall, insulation)
- Lights, trays, ballasts, fans, filters, air conditioner, water pumps
- Soil, nutrients, clones/seeds

Ongoing expenses
- Rent, electricity, water, nutrients, pesticides
- Refer to our Resource Section for a website that estimates operating costs of various grow lights.

Chapter 11 - Delivery Services

Depending on your location, due to city bans and moratoriums, a delivery service might be the only option for you to develop a collective. The laws on delivery-style collectives are less defined than those for traditional storefronts; in fact, more and more delivery services are popping up in towns where storefronts aren't allowed. Below is is a list of pros and cons of a delivery-style collective compared to a traditional storefront model.

Pros:
- Low start-up fees
- Lower overhead
- Fewer regulations, less bureaucracy
- Less attention from law enforcement
- Flexible schedule
- More nimble operations
- Can be discreet
- Some patients are immobile (don't have or can't operate vehicles)

Cons:
- Harder to get new members
- More competition
- No defined laws or guidelines
- Subjectivity by law enforcement
- Less security and higher potential for theft

"Delivery services are a relatively new creature, one that has not been directly addressed by the courts or in legislation," said Peter Krause, a California deputy attorney general who helped write the state's landmark guidelines on medical marijuana in 2008.[xxiv]

The same principals for starting and operating a storefront are required for a delivery service. Every member will need a valid doctor's recommendation and will need to sign the collective membership agreement, agreeing to follow the established bylaws. Both of these documents should be kept and filed in either hard copy or digital form. Ideally, you will keep a backup copy of these away from the originals in case of emergency.

A simple and efficient website can save you a lot of time and help streamline the processing of new members. Although not required, it is nice to have the option of an online pre-verification. It is here that potential members can scan in a copy of their doctor's recommendation, California ID, and perhaps even complete a membership agreement.

Safety should be your first concern when operating a delivery service. Depending on your location, you might require everyone to be pre-verified. Another option is to not allow members to buy medicine the day they sign up. With this procedure in place, the potential member will know you aren't likely to be carrying any money or product on you. This will allow you to obtain a photo of the member (via their ID) before any medicine is distributed, and because you have a copy of their ID, there will be less incentive to steal from you. Have the potential members bring a copy of their recommendation for you or bring a laptop and portable scanner with you to make a copy. With pre-verification, most of the paperwork can be handled ahead of time. Many patients, especially the elderly and those who are very sick, aren't very technically savvy, and it will be up to you to cater to them as well.

Carry only minimum amounts of cash and medicine on your person. Depending on the scope of your delivery area, it is a good idea to drop cash and re-stock your medicine multiple times a day. If you are commuting long distances, you should determine whether a second storage/drop location is needed.

It's a good idea to meet prospective members in public the first time. Although you won't want to meet people in certain public situations, it is comforting to know that others are around should you encounter a problem.

Some criminals view medical marijuana providers as easy targets because providers potentially have a lot of valuables, such as medicine and money, with them, and also because the chance of the provider calling the police is low because of the nature of the product. Storefront dispensaries typically employ a high level of security to ward off potential criminals, but delivery services don't have this same level of defense available to them. Always be vigilant, and don't put yourself in any dangerous situations. <u>Always remember that medicine and money are replaceable, but you are not.</u>

Chapter 12 – Federal MMJ Involvement

A New Approach for the Obama Administration (March 2009)

In March of 2009, after President Obama took office, federal Attorney General Eric H. Holder Jr. said the current administration was taking a new approach to federal drug laws and would end the frequent raids on distributors of medical marijuana that were commonplace during the Bush administration. Specifically, "Given the limited resources that we have, our focus will be on people, organizations that are growing, cultivating substantial amounts of marijuana and doing so in a way that's inconsistent with federal and state law."[xxv] Everyone in the medical marijuana industry felt this was a giant win. Finally, providers and patients could breathe easy, for a little while, at least.

Prop 19 (November 2010)

On Nov 2nd 2010 Californians voted on the legalization of marijuana for recreational use. U.S. Attorney General Eric Holder threatened to "vigorously enforce" federal marijuana laws even if California voters approved the ballot measure. In a letter to former Drug Enforcement Administration officials, Holder stated that "the Department of Justice strongly opposes Proposition 19." And if passed, he said, it "would provide a significant impediment to ... efforts by law enforcement to target drug traffickers who frequently distribute marijuana alongside cocaine and other controlled substances."

Unfortunately, Proposition 19 lost 46.2% to 53.8%, but that showed that a substantial number of Californians want change and feel that there are many positives that would come from legalization. Our fingers are crossed that a modified proposition for legalization will pass in the near future.

Federal Prosecutors Attack Property Owners (October 2011)

In early October, 2011, the federal government did an about-face. At a news conference in Sacramento, Andre Birotte Jr., the Los Angeles-based U.S. attorney for the Central District, stated that (his) Southern California region is home to the highest concentration of dispensaries in the nation. "We have yet to find a single instance in which a marijuana store was able to prove that it was a not-for-profit organization," he said.

"That is not what the California voters intended or authorized, and it is illegal under federal law," he said. "It does not allow this brick-and-mortar, Costco-Walmart-type model that we see across California."

California's four federal prosecutors also sent a number of letters to the property owners of these dispensaries, giving them two weeks to shut down. This same tactic was used by the Bush administration to successfully close a number of dispensaries in 2007. The feds can legally seize these properties through civil forfeiture if push comes to shove. According to the letters signed by U.S. Attorney Laura Duffy in San Diego, "Real and personal property involved in such operations are subject to seizure by and forfeiture to the United States ... regardless of the purported purpose of the dispensary." Luckily, most of the recently sent letters were nothing more than empty threats.[xxvi]

Federal Government Closes Down Dispensaries and Threatens To Seize Property (April 2012)

In April 2012, the DEA raided and shut down Oaksterdam University, the main medical cannabis industry trade school that was founded by Richard Lee in Oakland, California. A number of dispensaries and grow facilities were also raided in Southern California around that time. In early May of 2012, federal agents raided two dispensaries in Santa Barbara and issued cease and desist letters to the ten remaining dispensaries in town. These dispensaries were given two weeks to shut down or face criminal prosecution and the loss of property. The federal government stopped making threats and is attacking the marijuana industry at a previously unseen level.

According to Americans for Safe Access, since the Obama administration has been in office, they have unleashed an interagency cannabis crackdown that goes beyond anything seen under the Bush administration, with more than 100 raids, primarily on California pot dispensaries, many of them operating in full compliance with state laws. Since October 2009, the Justice Department has conducted more than 170 aggressive SWAT-style raids in 9 medical marijuana states, resulting in at least 61 federal indictments.

Federal Conclusion

The California medical marijuana industry has recently taken a step in the wrong direction, thanks to the recent federal encroachment. The federal government has filed property forfeiture lawsuits in a few instances where they are seeking the real property where medical marijuana was grown or sold. This occurred typically after warning letters were sent to the landlords. Fortunately, in most instances the feds are solely seizing marijuana, money and other contraband they find on-site and not pursuing criminal charges against the operators and directors of these facilities. It appears that the feds are trying to work through intimidation, as they don't have the time or resources to shut everyone down. So this is something you need to be aware of and do your best to stay out of their crosshairs.

Clandestine Operations

Given the recent actions of the federal government against medical marijuana providers, the lack of structured state guidelines, and varying opinions of local governments and law enforcement, some people may find it necessary and in their best interest to operate a low-profile operation. This might entail creating a delivery style operation rather than a storefront, limiting the size of the entity (number of members), not notifying the local government or law enforcement, not advertising, keeping accurate accounting records (secured off site), and basically trying to be an unnoticed collective of individuals. However, you will still have to be very careful to obey all state laws, and this will likely put added pressure on you to do so. Individuals will have to perform due diligence of their specific environment and make an overall assessment of their specific situation before starting a not-for-profit and partaking in any medical marijuana-related activities.

Chapter 13 - Encounters with Law Enforcement

The laws and attitudes regarding the cannabis plant are ever-changing. Currently in California, simple possession is an infraction. Still, there are people who will be unfortunate enough to have an unpleasant contact with law enforcement in connection with their legal medical marijuana. From our experience, here are some suggestions. First, always be polite. *Do not become belligerent.* It's one thing to calmly discuss your rights as an American citizen, and it's another thing when you act aggressively toward law enforcement. Usually there are three stages to the typical encounter: The first is questioning, the second is detaining, and the third is arrest.

Assume that any time you are talking to a police officer you are being recorded. If you are being investigated, the police officer will be wearing some type of wire or recording device.

Questioning Stage

This is where the police are trying to establish certain facts, such as why you are there or where you are going. If you answer at all, your explanations should be short and simple: "I'm going to my friend's house," "I'm here for dinner," and so on. If they continue to ask about things, then at some point you need to decide when you've given them enough information. That's when you start saying things like, "I'm not comfortable answering that question." Frequently, when challenged with non-answers, police will say, "Why? Do you have something to hide?" Politely answer, "I have nothing to hide but I want to invoke my right to remain silent," or something along those lines. At some point you need to ask, "Am I free to go?" Remember, if you do not ask to leave, they can continue to ask you questions. If you are not free to go they must have a reason for detaining you. Once you are not free to go, you are at the detained stage.

Detained Stage

This is the stage where you are technically in their custody and cannot leave until they say you can. They can search the outside of your clothes for weapons, and they may ask to search your vehicle, which you should always refuse. Remember that they must detain you for a reason, and the most frequent reason for reaching this stage is the smell of cannabis, which can lead to other revelations. If you are traveling with some cannabis that is not a quantity which could be reasonably assumed to be for personal use, you'd better have a good reason for transporting it. At this point in the process, most attorneys would advise a client to be polite but refuse to answer any more questions.

Arrest Stage

DO NOT TALK! KEEP YOUR MOUTH SHUT!

Completely innocent things you may say can be twisted later into incriminating statements. Do not think you can negotiate your way out. The police are evidence collectors; it is the district attorney who can negotiate with you. You can watch any number of police shows to see how people talk themselves into a jail cell. Get an attorney—those who resist communicating typically end up in the best situation.

In the end, if you should have an encounter, it is up to each individual whether they want to discuss their medical use or condition with law enforcement. Some people have health problems that they feel embarrassed to talk about. Just remember, if you are charged, under the law you are not required to reveal your health condition in court.

Acknowledgments

Mr. Restivo would like to thank God for everything he has been granted in his life. He also wants to send a special thank you to the lawyers he has worked with and learned from over the last few years: first and foremost, Allison Margolin and her team at Margolin & Lawrence, Gene Takagi at NOE Law Group, David Kohl and Eric D. Shevin, Esq. He also wants to thank William (Bill) Britt for his contribution and review of this guidebook – he is great man with an incredible knowledge of cannabis. Thanks to Michelle Restivo for her support, insight and editing. Thanks also to our professional editor, Lynn Stratton. Also, thanks to Chad Oxton, Eric Boone, Cory Cervantes and Warren Clark for giving up their valuable time to help finalize this book.

Final Thoughts:

You now have the information you need to get started in the California medical marijuana industry. As you probably have seen, there are some inherent risks involved, so be sure you weigh the pros and cons of your situation before you expend your time and money. This book should give you good insight into the challenges you are going to encounter running or growing for a dispensary. Unfortunately, the rules aren't clear-cut or simple. You will need to constantly stay in touch with current news and research case law and proposed local ordinances. Knowledge is mandatory in this industry, and you can never have too much. You can join a medical marijuana news site (like ours at www.californiadispensaryinfo.com) or blog to help you stay current on industry news.

Good Luck and Godspeed!

General Policies For Success:

- Incorporate and document your not-for-profit collective formation (containing your objectives). Follow through on corporate requirements, i.e., bylaws on-site, monthly board meetings, etc.

- Hire a good attorney or have one set up for emergencies.

- Make sure all members read and understand that they are members of a collective. (Imagine that every member is or could be an informant.) Allow only members within the dispensary, and be sure that all doctors' recommendations have been verified and kept current – no exceptions.

- Keep clean, detailed accounting and reimbursement records, preferably backed up off-site. Be transparent.

- Keep wages reasonable – The board of directors should approve and document their reasoning .

- Use a small number of trusted collective growers if the BOD and employees can't produce it all.

- Create an emergency plan of action (for robberies, raids, etc.).

- Don't keep guns at medical marijuana grow sites, collectives, or anywhere else they could be connected to these activities.

- Follow all the requirements of a normal business (i.e., sales, payroll, and property taxes).

- Don't take short-cuts when starting the collective or complying with regulations.

- Make friends in the community.

- Stay current with local, state and federal laws, and attend city council meetings.

- Have respect for the neighbors and community in general.

Resources

Visit our website at www.californiadispensaryinfo.com for additional information, including sample collective bylaws, cultivation agreement, and board of directors' minutes (use password "prop215" for access). We will also provide law updates and current MMJ news.

MMJ Organizations to be involved with:
a. Americans for Safe Access - http://safeaccessnow.org/
b. National Organization for the Reform of Marijuana Laws - http://norml.org

Service and Product Providers

Breeze Insurance Services, Scott Sherwood (760) 717-1069
http://www.scottsherwoodins.com

Cal Canna Labs – Marijuana testing/quality control Jake Quinn (858) 461-8378
http://www.calcannalabs.com/

Excellent MMJ patient database management system (MMJOS), Steve (575) 779-0684
www.mmjos.com/index.php?x=jr

Sunrise Technology (Point of Sale System) Nathaniel Stacker, (714) 444-2844 (ext 30)
http://sunrisepos.com/

The Transaction Group (CC Processing) Michael Rupkalvis (904) 685-8331
http://www.thetransactiongroup.net/

Other Resources

BOE – marijuana sales (June 2007)
http://www.boe.ca.gov/news/pdf/173.pdf

BOE rates
http://www.boe.ca.gov/cgi-bin/rates.cgi

CA Medical Marijuana Program
http://www.cdph.ca.gov/programs/MMP/Pages/MedicalMarijuanaProgram.aspx

CA Secretary of State Business Portal
http://www.sos.ca.gov/business/

CA Law
http://www.leginfo.ca.gov/calaw.html

CA Department of Industrial Relations – Posting requirements
http://www.dir.ca.gov/wpnodb.html

Franchise Tax Board - California Corporations Tax Booklet
http://www.ftb.ca.gov/forms/2010/10_100bk.pdf

Grow light operating cost – GreenTree Hydroponics
http://www.hydroponics.net/learn/hid_lamp_op_cost.asp

HIPAA Laws
http://www.hhs.gov/ocr/privacy/

Legal information – Self help
www.nolo.com

Marijuana Strains
http://www.medicalmarijuanastrains.com/category/cannabis-sativa/

<u>Additional Cooperative Information</u>

i. National Cooperative Business Association
http://www.ncba.coop/ncba/home

ii. Co-ops USA
http://www.co-opsusa.coop/

iii. California Center for Cooperative Development
http://www.cccd.coop/

FULL Disclosure:

We have provided a number of references in this book and we feel confident in all of them. A few of them are aware of this guidebook and have offered to provide you with discounts and referral credit for us. Please let these companies know how you found out about them—and thanks☺

Endnotes

[i]Prop 215 (H&S Code 11262.5), CA Department of Health, State of California, January 21, 2011,
http://www.cdph.ca.gov/programs/MMP/Pages/CompassionateUseact.aspx

State of California, Health and Safety Code, January 21, 2011,
http://www.leginfo.ca.gov/cgi-bin/displaycode?section=hsc&group=11001-12000&file=11362.7-11362.83

[ii]Medical Marijuana Program (SB 420), CA Department of Health, State of California, December 19, 2010
http://www.cdph.ca.gov/programs/MMP/Pages/Medical%20Marijuana%20Program.aspx

[iii]Kamala Harris, 12/21/11 Letter Re: Medical Marijuana Guidelines, State of California, February 3, 2012
http://ag.ca.gov/cms_attachments/press/pdfs/n2600_letter_a2.pdf

[iv]Wikipedia, "Collective" definition, Wikipedia Foundation, Inc., June, 16 2011
http://en.wikipedia.org/wiki/Collective

[v]Barons Law Dictionary, "Cooperative Association" definition, Answers Corporation, June 16, 2011
http://www.answers.com/topic/cooperative-association#ixzz1XmA4wsni

[vi]Got Weed Blog, "Cooperative cultivation" definition, GotWeedWordpress.com, June 17, 2011
http://gotweed.wordpress.com/2009/06/20/compassionate-care-guidelines-for-dispensaries-collectives-and-cooperatives-from-the-california-attorney-general-august-2008/

[vii]Supreme Court of California, People v. Mentch, FindLaw, January 21, 2011
http://caselaw.findlaw.com/ca-supreme-court/1312188.html

[viii]eHow.com, What Does Agent for Service of Process Mean?, Demand Media, January 15, 2012
http://www.ehow.com/facts_5760060_agent-service-process-mean_.html#ixzz1ndVL35uE

[ix] California Secretary of State, Organization of California Nonprofit, Nonstock Corporations, State of California, March 15, 2011
http://www.sos.ca.gov/business/corp/pdf/articles/corp_artsnp.pdf

[x] Wikipedia, "By-law" definition, Wikipedia Foundation, Inc., December, 22 2011
http://en.wikipedia.org/wiki/Bylaw

[xi] Nolo.com, How to Form a California Nonprofit Corporation, Nolo.com, December 22, 2011
http://www.nolo.com/legal-encyclopedia/forming-nonprofit-corporation-california-36053.html

[xii] Nolo.com, Documenting Corporate Decisions, Nolo.com, December 22, 2011
http://www.nolo.com/legal-encyclopedia/documenting-corporate-decisions-29503.html

[xiii] Nolo.com, Documenting Corporate Decisions, Nolo.com, December 22, 2011
http://www.nolo.com/legal-encyclopedia/documenting-corporate-decisions-29503.html

[xiv] Guidestar.com, Director's Compensation, Guidestar.com, June 16, 2011
http://www2.guidestar.org/

[xv] eHow.com, HIPAA Privacy Laws, eHow.com, Jan 5, 2012
HIPAA Privacy Laws | eHow.com http://www.ehow.com/facts_4968352_hipaa-privacy-laws.html#ixzz1mO4Pz1x9

[xvi] Patients' Marijuana, Marijuana Strains (the basics), Patients' Marijuana, January 16, 2012
http://www.patientsmarijuana.org/faqs.html

[xvii] IRS Section 280E, Expenditures in Connection with the Illegal Sales of Drugs, U.S. Department of the Treasury, Via Cornell University Law School, Dec 22, 2011
http://www.law.cornell.edu/uscode/text/26/280E

[xviii] U.S. Tax Court, Californians Helping to Alleviate Medical Problems, Inc. , Petitioner v. Commissioner of the Internal Revenue, Respondent, U.S. Government, Dec 22, 2011
http://www.ustaxcourt.gov/InOpHistoric/champ.TC.WPD.pdf

[xix]Department of Homeland Security, Form I-9 Employment Eligibility Verification, U.S. Citizenship and Immigration Services Sept 28, 2011 http://www.uscis.gov/files/form/i-9.pdf

[xx]California Dept. of Industrial Relations, CAL/OSHA Industry Guides, State of California, September 30, 2011 http://www.dir.ca.gov/dosh/puborder.asp

[xxi]Americans for Safe Access, Medical Marijuana Edibles and the Law, Americans for Safe Access, September 30, 2011 http://www.safeaccessnow.org/downloads/June%20Southern%20California%20ASA%20Calendar.pdf

[xxii]Cal Canna Labs (San Diego),Why Test Medical Marijuana in a Lab for Potency or Pesticides?, Cal Canna Labs.com January 15, 2012 http://www.calcannalabs.com/

[xxiii]Clean Green Certification, Medical Cannabis Certification for Growers, Clean Green Certification, January 15, 2011 http://cleangreencert.com/

[xxiv]Gary Cohn and Michael Montgomery, Marijuana delivery services evade ban on dispensaries, spreading across California, California Watch, June 16, 2011 http://californiawatch.org/public-safety/marijuana-delivery-services-evade-bans-dispensaries-spreading-across-california

[xxv]David W. Ogden, Memorandum For Selected United States Attorneys – Investigations and Prosecutions in States Authorizing Medical Use of Marijuana, US Department of Justice, January 21, 2011 http://www.justice.gov/opa/documents/medical-marijuana.pdf

[xxvi] John Hoeffel, Federal crackdown on medical pot sales reflect a shift in policy, Los Angeles Times, January 23, 2011 http://articles.latimes.com/2011/oct/07/local/la-me-obama-medical-marijuana-20111008

Marijuana Policy Project, Federal Enforcement Policy De-Prioritizing Medical Marijuana Statements from Pres. Obama, his spokesman, and the Justice Department, Marijuana Policy Project, Jan 21, 2011 http://www.mpp.org/assets/pdfs/library/HolderObamaStatements.pdf

Chris Roberts, Blowing Smoke: Obama Promises One Thing, Does Another on Medical Marijuana, SFWeekly, June, 26 2011 http://www.sfweekly.com/2011-04-06/news/medical-marijuana-raids-obama-eric-holder-legalization-dispensaries-chris-roberts/

ATTACHMENT 1

EDMUND G. BROWN JR
Attorney General

DEPARTMENT OF JUSTICE
State of California

GUIDELINES FOR THE SECURITY AND NON-DIVERSION
OF MARIJUANA GROWN FOR MEDICAL USE
August 2008

In 1996, California voters approved an initiative that exempted certain patients and their primary caregivers from criminal liability under state law for the possession and cultivation of marijuana. In 2003, the Legislature enacted additional legislation relating to medical marijuana. One of those statutes requires the Attorney General to adopt "guidelines to ensure the security and nondiversion of marijuana grown for medical use." (Health & Saf. Code, § 11362.81(d).[1]) To fulfill this mandate, this Office is issuing the following guidelines to (1) ensure that marijuana grown for medical purposes remains secure and does not find its way to non-patients or illicit markets, (2) help law enforcement agencies perform their duties effectively and in accordance with California law, and (3) help patients and primary caregivers understand how they may cultivate, transport, possess, and use medical marijuana under California law.

I.   SUMMARY OF APPLICABLE LAW

A.   California Penal Provisions Relating to Marijuana.

The possession, sale, cultivation, or transportation of marijuana is ordinarily a crime under California law. (See, e.g., § 11357 [possession of marijuana is a misdemeanor]; § 11358 [cultivation of marijuana is a felony]; Veh. Code, § 23222 [possession of less than 1 oz. of marijuana while driving is a misdemeanor]; § 11359 [possession with intent to sell any amount of marijuana is a felony]; § 11360 [transporting, selling, or giving away marijuana in California is a felony; under 28.5 grams is a misdemeanor]; § 11361 [selling or distributing marijuana to minors, or using a minor to transport, sell, or give away marijuana, is a felony].)

---

[1] Unless otherwise noted, all statutory references are to the Health & Safety Code.

B.   Proposition 215 - The Compassionate Use Act of 1996.

On November 5, 1996, California voters passed Proposition 215, which decriminalized the cultivation and use of marijuana by seriously ill individuals upon a physician's recommendation. (§ 11362.5.) Proposition 215 was enacted to "ensure that seriously ill Californians have the right to obtain and use marijuana for medical purposes where that medical use is deemed appropriate and has been recommended by a physician who has determined that the person's health would benefit from the use of marijuana," and to "ensure that patients and their primary caregivers who obtain and use marijuana for medical purposes upon the recommendation of a physician are not subject to criminal prosecution or sanction." (§ 11362.5(b)(1)(A)-(B).)

The Act further states that "Section 11357, relating to the possession of marijuana, and Section 11358, relating to the cultivation of marijuana, shall not apply to a patient, or to a patient's primary caregiver, who possesses or cultivates marijuana for the personal medical purposes of the patient upon the written or verbal recommendation or approval of a physician." (§ 11362.5(d).) Courts have found an implied defense to the transportation of medical marijuana when the "quantity transported and the method, timing and distance of the transportation are reasonably related to the patient's current medical needs." (People v. Trippet (1997) 56 Cal.App.4th 1532, 1551.)

C.   Senate Bill 420 - The Medical Marijuana Program Act.

On January 1, 2004, Senate Bill 420, the Medical Marijuana Program Act (MMP), became law. (§§ 11362.7-11362.83.) The MMP, among other things, requires the California Department of Public Health (DPH) to establish and maintain a program for the voluntary registration of qualified medical marijuana patients and their primary caregivers through a statewide identification card system. Medical marijuana identification cards are intended to help law enforcement officers identify and verify that cardholders are able to cultivate, possess, and transport certain amounts of marijuana without being subject to arrest under specific conditions. (§§ 11362.71(e), 11362.78.)

It is mandatory that all counties participate in the identification card program by:
   (a.) providing applications upon request to individuals seeking to join the identification card program;
   (b.) processing completed applications;
      (a.) maintaining certain records;

(b.) following state implementation protocols; and (e) issuing DPH identification cards to approved applicants and designated primary caregivers. (§ 11362.71(b).)

Participation by patients and primary caregivers in the identification card program is voluntary. However, because identification cards offer the holder protection from arrest, are issued only after verification of the cardholder's status as a qualified patient or primary caregiver, and are immediately verifiable online or via telephone, they represent one of the best ways to ensure the security and non-diversion of marijuana grown for medical use.

In addition to establishing the identification card program, the MMP also defines certain terms, sets possession guidelines for cardholders, and recognizes a qualified right to collective and cooperative cultivation of medical marijuana. (§§ 11362.7, 11362.77, 11362.775.)

D. Taxability of Medical Marijuana Transactions.

In February 2007, the California State Board of Equalization (BOE) issued a Special Notice confirming its policy of taxing medical marijuana transactions, as well as its requirement that businesses engaging in such transactions hold a Seller's Permit. (http://www.boe.ca.gov/news/pdf/medseller2007.pdf) According to the Notice, having a Seller's Permit does not allow individuals to make unlawful sales, but instead merely provides a way to remit any sales and use taxes due. BOE further clarified its policy in a June 2007 Special Notice that addressed several frequently asked questions concerning taxation of medical marijuana transactions. (http://www.boe.ca.gov/news/pdf/173.pdf.)

E. Medical Board of California.

The Medical Board of California licenses, investigates, and disciplines California physicians. (Bus. & Prof. Code, § 2000, et seq.) Although state law prohibits punishing a physician simply for recommending marijuana for treatment of a serious medical condition (§ 11362.5(c)), the Medical Board can and does take disciplinary action against physicians who fail to comply with accepted medical standards when recommending marijuana. In a May 13, 2004 press release, the Medical Board clarified that these accepted standards are the same ones that a reasonable and prudent physician would follow when recommending or approving any medication. They include the following:

1. Taking a history and conducting a good faith examination of the patient;
2. Developing a treatment plan with objectives;

3. Providing informed consent, including discussion of side effects;
4. Periodically reviewing the treatment's efficacy;
5. Consultations, as necessary; and
6. Keeping proper records supporting the decision to recommend the use of medical marijuana.
   (http://www.mbc.ca.gov/board/media/releases_2004_05-13_marijuana.html.)

Complaints about physicians should be addressed to the Medical Board (1-800-633-2322 or www.mbc.ca.gov), which investigates and prosecutes alleged licensing violations in conjunction with the Attorney General's Office.

F.   The Federal Controlled Substances Act.

Adopted in 1970, the Controlled Substances Act (CSA) established a federal regulatory system designed to combat recreational drug abuse by making it unlawful to manufacture, distribute, dispense, or possess any controlled substance. (21 U.S.C. § 801, et seq.; Gonzales v. Oregon (2006) 546 U.S. 243, 271-273.) The CSA reflects the federal government's view that marijuana is a drug with "no currently accepted medical use." (21 U.S.C. § 812(b)(1).) Accordingly, the manufacture, distribution, or possession of marijuana is a federal criminal offense. (Id. at §§ 841(a)(1), 844(a).)

The incongruity between federal and state law has given rise to understandable confusion, but no legal conflict exists merely because state law and federal law treat marijuana differently. Indeed, California's medical marijuana laws have been challenged unsuccessfully in court on the ground that they are preempted by the CSA. (County of San Diego v. San Diego NORML (July 31, 2008) --- Cal.Rptr.3d ---, 2008 WL 2930117.) Congress has provided that states are free to regulate in the area of controlled substances, including marijuana, provided that state law does not positively conflict with the CSA. (21 U.S.C. § 903.) Neither Proposition 215, nor the MMP, conflict with the CSA because, in adopting these laws, California did not "legalize" medical marijuana, but instead exercised the state's reserved powers to not punish certain marijuana offenses under state law when a physician has recommended its use to treat a serious medical condition. (See City of Garden Grove v. Superior Court (Kha) (2007) 157 Cal.App.4th 355, 371-373, 381-382.)

In light of California's decision to remove the use and cultivation of physician-recommended marijuana from the scope of the state's drug laws, this Office recommends that state and local law enforcement officers not arrest individuals or seize marijuana under federal law when the officer determines from the facts available that the cultivation, possession, or transportation is permitted under California's medical marijuana laws.

II. DEFINITIONS

A. **Physician's Recommendation:** Physicians may not prescribe marijuana because the federal Food and Drug Administration regulates prescription drugs and, under the CSA, marijuana is a Schedule I drug, meaning that it has no recognized medical use. Physicians may, however, lawfully issue a verbal or written recommendation under California law indicating that marijuana would be a beneficial treatment for a serious medical condition. (§ 11362.5(d); Conant v. Walters (9th Cir. 2002) 309 F.3d 629, 632.)

B. **Primary Caregiver:** A primary caregiver is a person who is designated by a qualified patient and "has consistently assumed responsibility for the housing, health, or safety" of the patient. (§ 11362.5(e).) California courts have emphasized the consistency element of the patient-caregiver relationship. Although a "primary caregiver who consistently grows and supplies . . . medicinal marijuana for a section 11362.5 patient is serving a health need of the patient," someone who merely maintains a source of marijuana does not automatically become the party "who has consistently assumed responsibility for the housing, health, or safety" of that purchaser. (People ex rel. Lungren v. Peron (1997) 59 Cal.App.4th 1383, 1390, 1400.) A person may serve as primary caregiver to "more than one" patient, provided that the patients and caregiver all reside in the same city or county. (§ 11362.7(d)(2).) Primary caregivers also may receive certain compensation for their services. (§ 11362.765(c) ["A primary caregiver who receives compensation for actual expenses, including reasonable compensation incurred for services provided . . . to enable [a patient] to use marijuana under this article, or for payment for out-of-pocket expenses incurred in providing those services, or both, . . . shall not, on the sole basis of that fact, be subject to prosecution" for possessing or transporting marijuana].)

C. **Qualified Patient:** A qualified patient is a person whose physician has recommended the use of marijuana to treat a serious illness, including cancer, anorexia, AIDS, chronic pain, spasticity, glaucoma, arthritis, migraine, or any other illness for which marijuana provides relief. (§ 11362.5(b)(1)(A).)

Recommending Physician: A recommending physician is a person who (1) possesses a license in good standing to practice medicine in California; (2) has taken responsibility for some aspect of the medical care, treatment, diagnosis, counseling, or referral of a patient; and (3) has complied with accepted medical standards (as described by the Medical Board of California in its May 13, 2004 press release) that a reasonable and prudent physician would follow when recommending or approving medical marijuana for the treatment of his or her patient.

III. GUIDELINES REGARDING INDIVIDUAL QUALIFIED PATIENTS AND PRIMARY CAREGIVERS

A. State Law Compliance Guidelines.

1. **Physician Recommendation:** Patients must have a written or verbal recommendation for medical marijuana from a licensed physician. (§ 11362.5(d).)

2. **State of California Medical Marijuana Identification Card:** Under the MMP, qualified patients and their primary caregivers may voluntarily apply for a card issued by DPH identifying them as a person who is authorized to use, possess, or transport marijuana grown for medical purposes. To help law enforcement officers verify the cardholder's identity, each card bears a unique identification number, and a verification database is available online (www.calmmp.ca.gov). In addition, the cards contain the name of the county health department that approved the application, a 24-hour verification telephone number, and an expiration date. (§§ 11362.71(a); 11362.735(a)(3)-(4); 11362.745.)

3. **Proof of Qualified Patient Status:** Although verbal recommendations are technically permitted under Proposition 215, patients should obtain and carry written proof of their physician recommendations to help them avoid arrest. A state identification card is the best form of proof, because it is easily verifiable and provides immunity from arrest if certain conditions are met (see section III.B.4, below). The next best forms of proof are a city- or county-issued patient identification card, or a written recommendation from a physician.

4. **Possession Guidelines**:

a) **MMP:**[2] Qualified patients and primary caregivers who possess a state-issued identification card may possess 8 oz. of dried marijuana, and may maintain no more than 6 mature or 12 immature plants per qualified patient. (§ 11362.77(a).) But, if "a qualified patient or primary caregiver has a doctor's recommendation that this quantity does not meet the qualified patient's medical needs, the qualified patient or primary caregiver may possess an amount of marijuana consistent with the patient's needs." (§ 11362.77(b).) Only the dried mature processed flowers or buds of the female cannabis plant should be considered when determining allowable quantities of medical marijuana for purposes of the MMP. (§ 11362.77(d).)

b) **Local Possession Guidelines:** Counties and cities may adopt regulations that allow qualified patients or primary caregivers to possess medical marijuana in amounts that exceed the MMP's possession guidelines. (§ 11362.77(c).)

c) **Proposition 215:** Qualified patients claiming protection under Proposition 215 may possess an amount of marijuana that is "reasonably related to [their] current medical needs." (People v. Trippet (1997) 56 Cal.App.4th 1532, 1549.)

B. **Enforcement Guidelines.**

1. **Location of Use:** Medical marijuana may not be smoked (a) where smoking is prohibited by law, (b) at or within 1000 feet of a school, recreation center, or youth center (unless the medical use occurs within a residence), (c) on a school bus, or (d) in a moving motor vehicle or boat. (§ 11362.79.)

---

[2] On May 22, 2008, California's Second District Court of Appeal severed Health & Safety Code § 11362.77 from the MMP on the ground that the statute's possession guidelines were an unconstitutional amendment of Proposition 215, which does not quantify the marijuana a patient may possess. (See People v. Kelly (2008) 163 Cal.App.4th 124, 77 Cal.Rptr.3d 390.) The Third District Court of Appeal recently reached a similar conclusion in People v. Phomphakdy (July 31, 2008) --- Cal.Rptr.3d ---, 2008 WL 2931369. The California Supreme Court has granted review in Kelly and the Attorney General intends to seek review in Phomphakdy.

2. **Use of Medical Marijuana in the Workplace or at Correctional Facilities:** The medical use of marijuana need not be accommodated in the workplace, during work hours, or at any jail, correctional facility, or other penal institution. (§ 11362.785(a); Ross v. RagingWire Telecomms., Inc. (2008) 42 Cal.4th 920, 933 [under the Fair Employment and Housing Act, an employer may terminate an employee who tests positive for marijuana use].)

3. **Criminal Defendants, Probationers, and Parolees:** Criminal defendants and probationers may request court approval to use medical marijuana while they are released on bail or probation. The court's decision and reasoning must be stated on the record and in the minutes of the court. Likewise, parolees who are eligible to use medical marijuana may request that they be allowed to continue such use during the period of parole. The written conditions of parole must reflect whether the request was granted or denied. (§ 11362.795.)

4. **State of California Medical Marijuana Identification Cardholders:** When a person invokes the protections of Proposition 215 or the MMP and he or she possesses a state medical marijuana identification card, officers should:

   a) Review the identification card and verify its validity either by calling the telephone number printed on the card, or by accessing DPH's card verification website (http://www.calmmp.ca.gov); and

   b) If the card is valid and not being used fraudulently, there are no other indicia of illegal activity (weapons, illicit drugs, or excessive amounts of cash), and the person is within the state or local possession guidelines, the individual should be released and the marijuana should not be seized. Under the MMP, "no person or designated primary caregiver in possession of a valid state medical marijuana identification card shall be subject to arrest for possession, transportation, delivery, or cultivation of medical marijuana." (§ 11362.71(e).) Further, a "state or local law enforcement agency or officer shall not refuse to accept an identification card issued by the department unless the state or local law enforcement agency or officer has reasonable cause to believe that the information contained in the card is false or fraudulent, or the card is being used fraudulently." (§ 11362.78.)

5. Non-Cardholders: When a person claims protection under Proposition 215 or the MMP and only has a locally issued (i.e., non-state) patient identification card, or a written (or verbal) recommendation from a licensed physician, officers should use their sound professional judgment to assess the validity of the person's medical-use claim:

a) Officers need not abandon their search or investigation. The standard search and seizure rules apply to the enforcement of marijuana-related violations. Reasonable suspicion is required for detention, while probable cause is required for search, seizure, and arrest.

b) Officers should review any written documentation for validity. It may contain the physician's name, telephone number, address, and license number.

c) If the officer reasonably believes that the medical-use claim is valid based upon the totality of the circumstances (including the quantity of marijuana, packaging for sale, the presence of weapons, illicit drugs, or large amounts of cash), and the person is within the state or local possession guidelines or has an amount consistent with their current medical needs, the person should be released and the marijuana should not be seized.

d) Alternatively, if the officer has probable cause to doubt the validity of a person's medical marijuana claim based upon the facts and circumstances, the person may be arrested and the marijuana may be seized. It will then be up to the person to establish his or her medical marijuana defense in court.

e) Officers are not obligated to accept a person's claim of having a verbal physician's recommendation that cannot be readily verified with the physician at the time of detention.

6. Exceeding Possession Guidelines: If a person has what appears to be valid medical marijuana documentation, but exceeds the applicable possession guidelines identified above, all marijuana may be seized.

7. Return of Seized Medical Marijuana: If a person whose marijuana is seized by law enforcement successfully establishes a medical marijuana defense in court, or the case is not prosecuted, he or she

may file a motion for return of the marijuana. If a court grants the motion and orders the return of marijuana seized incident to an arrest, the individual or entity subject to the order must return the property. State law enforcement officers who handle controlled substances in the course of their official duties are immune from liability under the CSA. (21 U.S.C. § 885(d).) Once the marijuana is returned, federal authorities are free to exercise jurisdiction over it. (21 U.S.C. §§ 812(c)(10), 844(a); City of Garden Grove v. Superior Court (Kha) (2007) 157 Cal.App.4th 355, 369, 386, 391.)

IV. GUIDELINES REGARDING COLLECTIVES AND COOPERATIVES

Under California law, medical marijuana patients and primary caregivers may "associate within the State of California in order collectively or cooperatively to cultivate marijuana for medical purposes." (§ 11362.775.) The following guidelines are meant to apply to qualified patients and primary caregivers who come together to collectively or cooperatively cultivate physician-recommended marijuana.

A. **Business Forms:** Any group that is collectively or cooperatively cultivating and distributing marijuana for medical purposes should be organized and operated in a manner that ensures the security of the crop and safeguards against diversion for non-medical purposes. The following are guidelines to help cooperatives and collectives operate within the law, and to help law enforcement determine whether they are doing so.

1. **Statutory Cooperatives:** A cooperative must file articles of incorporation with the state and conduct its business for the mutual benefit of its members. (Corp. Code, § 12201, 12300.) No business may call itself a "cooperative" (or "co-op") unless it is properly organized and registered as such a corporation under the Corporations or Food and Agricultural Code. (Id. at § 12311(b).) Cooperative corporations are "democratically controlled and are not organized to make a profit for themselves, as such, or for their members, as such, but primarily for their members as patrons." (Id. at § 12201.) The earnings and savings of the business must be used for the general welfare of its members or equitably distributed to members in the form of cash, property, credits, or services. (Ibid.) Cooperatives must follow strict rules on organization, articles, elections, and distribution of earnings, and must report individual transactions from individual

members each year. (See id. at § 12200, et seq.) Agricultural cooperatives are likewise nonprofit corporate entities "since they are not organized to make profit for themselves, as such, or for their members, as such, but only for their members as producers." (Food & Agric. Code, § 54033.) Agricultural cooperatives share many characteristics with consumer cooperatives. (See, e.g., id. at § 54002, et seq.) Cooperatives should not purchase marijuana from, or sell to, non-members; instead, they should only provide a means for facilitating or coordinating transactions between members.

2. **Collectives:** California law does not define collectives, but the dictionary defines them as "a business, farm, etc., jointly owned and operated by the members of a group." (Random House Unabridged Dictionary; Random House, Inc. © 2006.) Applying this definition, a collective should be an organization that merely facilitates the collaborative efforts of patient and caregiver members – including the allocation of costs and revenues. As such, a collective is not a statutory entity, but as a practical matter it might have to organize as some form of business to carry out its activities. The collective should not purchase marijuana from, or sell to, non-members; instead, it should only provide a means for facilitating or coordinating transactions between members.

B. **Guidelines for the Lawful Operation of a Cooperative or Collective:** Collectives and cooperatives should be organized with sufficient structure to ensure security, non-diversion of marijuana to illicit markets, and compliance with all state and local laws. The following are some suggested guidelines and practices for operating collective growing operations to help ensure lawful operation.

1. **Non-Profit Operation:** Nothing in Proposition 215 or the MMP authorizes collectives, cooperatives, or individuals to profit from the sale or distribution of marijuana. (See, e.g., § 11362.765(a) ["nothing in this section shall authorize . . . any individual or group to cultivate or distribute marijuana for profit"].)

2. **Business Licenses, Sales Tax, and Seller's Permits:** The State Board of Equalization has determined that medical marijuana transactions are subject to sales tax, regardless of whether the individual or group makes a profit, and those engaging in transactions involving medical marijuana must obtain a Seller's Permit. Some cities and counties also require dispensing collectives and cooperatives to obtain business

licenses.

3. **Membership Application and Verification:** When a patient or primary caregiver wishes to join a collective or cooperative, the group can help prevent the diversion of marijuana for non-medical use by having potential members complete a written membership application. The following application guidelines should be followed to help ensure that marijuana grown for medical use is not diverted to illicit markets:

   a) Verify the individual's status as a qualified patient or primary caregiver. Unless he or she has a valid state medical marijuana identification card, this should involve personal contact with the recommending physician (or his or her agent), verification of the physician's identity, as well as his or her state licensing status. Verification of primary caregiver status should include contact with the qualified patient, as well as validation of the patient's recommendation. Copies should be made of the physician's recommendation or identification card, if any;

   b) Have the individual agree not to distribute marijuana to non-members;

   c) Have the individual agree not to use the marijuana for other than medical purposes;

   d) Maintain membership records on-site or have them reasonably available;

   e) Track when members' medical marijuana recommendation and/or identification cards expire; and

   f) Enforce conditions of membership by excluding members whose identification card or physician recommendation are invalid or have expired, or who are caught diverting marijuana for non-medical use.

4. **Collectives Should Acquire, Possess, and Distribute Only Lawfully Cultivated Marijuana:** Collectives and cooperatives should acquire marijuana only from their constituent members, because only marijuana grown by a qualified patient or his or her primary caregiver may lawfully be transported by, or distributed to, other members of a collective or cooperative. (§§ 11362.765, 11362.775.) The collective or cooperative may then allocate it to other members of the group. Nothing allows marijuana to be purchased from outside the collective or cooperative for distribution to its members. Instead, the cycle should be a closed- circuit of marijuana cultivation and consumption with no purchases or sales to or from non-members. To help prevent

diversion of medical marijuana to non- medical markets, collectives and cooperatives should document each member's contribution of labor, resources, or money to the enterprise. They also should track and record the source of their marijuana.

5. **Distribution and Sales to Non-Members are Prohibited:** State law allows primary caregivers to be reimbursed for certain services (including marijuana cultivation), but nothing allows individuals or groups to sell or distribute marijuana to non-members. Accordingly, a collective or cooperative may not distribute medical marijuana to any person who is not a member in good standing of the organization. A dispensing collective or cooperative may credit its members for marijuana they provide to the collective, which it may then allocate to other members. (§ 11362.765(c).) Members also may reimburse the collective or cooperative for marijuana that has been allocated to them. Any monetary reimbursement that members provide to the collective or cooperative should only be an amount necessary to cover overhead costs and operating expenses.

6. **Permissible Reimbursements and Allocations:** Marijuana grown at a collective or cooperative for medical purposes may be:

   a) Provided free to qualified patients and primary caregivers who are members of the collective or cooperative;
   b) Provided in exchange for services rendered to the entity;
   c) Allocated based on fees that are reasonably calculated to cover overhead costs and operating expenses; or
   d) Any combination of the above.

7. **Possession and Cultivation Guidelines:** If a person is acting as primary caregiver to more than one patient under section 11362.7(d)(2), he or she may aggregate the possession and cultivation limits for each patient. For example, applying the MMP's basic possession guidelines, if a caregiver is responsible for three patients, he or she may possess up to 24 oz. of marijuana (8 oz. per patient) and may grow 18 mature or 36 immature plants. Similarly, collectives and cooperatives may cultivate and transport marijuana in aggregate amounts tied to its membership numbers. Any patient or primary caregiver exceeding individual possession guidelines should have supporting records readily available when:
   a) Operating a location for cultivation;

b) Transporting the group's medical marijuana; and

c) Operating a location for distribution to members of the collective or cooperative.

8. **Security:** Collectives and cooperatives should provide adequate security to ensure that patients are safe and that the surrounding homes or businesses are not negatively impacted by nuisance activity such as loitering or crime. Further, to maintain security, prevent fraud, and deter robberies, collectives and cooperatives should keep accurate records and follow accepted cash handling practices, including regular bank runs and cash drops, and maintain a general ledger of cash transactions.

C.   **Enforcement Guidelines:** Depending upon the facts and circumstances, deviations from the guidelines outlined above, or other indicia that marijuana is not for medical use, may give rise to probable cause for arrest and seizure. The following are additional guidelines to help identify medical marijuana collectives and cooperatives that are operating outside of state law.

1.   **Storefront Dispensaries:** Although medical marijuana "dispensaries" have been operating in California for years, dispensaries, as such, are not recognized under the law. As noted above, the only recognized group entities are cooperatives and collectives. (§ 11362.775.) It is the opinion of this Office that a properly organized and operated collective or cooperative that dispenses medical marijuana through a storefront may be lawful under California law, but that dispensaries that do not substantially comply with the guidelines set forth in sections IV(A) and (B), above, are likely operating outside the protections of Proposition 215 and the MMP, and that the individuals operating such entities may be subject to arrest and criminal prosecution under California law. For example, dispensaries that merely require patients to complete a form summarily designating the business owner as their primary caregiver – and then offering marijuana in exchange for cash "donations" – are likely unlawful. (Peron, supra, 59 Cal.App.4th at p. 1400 [cannabis club owner was not the primary caregiver to thousands of patients where he did not consistently assume responsibility for their housing, health, or safety].)

2. **Indicia of Unlawful Operation:** When investigating collectives or cooperatives, law enforcement officers should be alert for signs of mass production or illegal sales, including (a) excessive amounts of marijuana, (b) excessive amounts of cash, (c) failure to follow local and state laws applicable to similar businesses, such as maintenance of any required licenses and payment of any required taxes, including sales taxes, (d) weapons, (e) illicit drugs, (f) purchases from, or sales or distribution to, non-members, or (g) distribution outside of California.

ATTACHMENT 2

MUTUAL BENEFIT SAMPLE

Articles of Incorporation

I

The name of the corporation is _____ *[Name of Corporation]*

II

A. This corporation is a nonprofit Mutual Benefit Corporation organized under the Nonprofit Mutual Benefit Corporation Law. The purpose of this corporation is to engage in any lawful act or activity, other than credit union business, for which a corporation may be organized under such law.

B. The specific purpose of this corporation is to _____

III

The name and address in the State of California of this corporation's initial agent for service of process is:

Name _____

Address _____

City _____ State **CALIFORNIA** Zip Code _____

IV

Notwithstanding any of the above statements of purposes and powers, this corporation shall not, except to an insubstantial degree, engage in any activities or exercise any powers that are not in furtherance of the specific purposes of this corporation.

_____
[Signature of Incorporator]
[Type Name of Incorporator], Incorporator

If an individual is designated as the initial agent for service of process, include the agent's business or residential street address in California (a P.O. Box address is not acceptable). If another corporation is designated as the initial agent for service of process, do not include the address of the designated corporation.

This sample should be used ONLY as a guideline in the preparation of the original document for filing with the California Secretary of State.

Secretary of State Sample
ARTS-MU (REV 04/2010)

ATTACHMENT 3

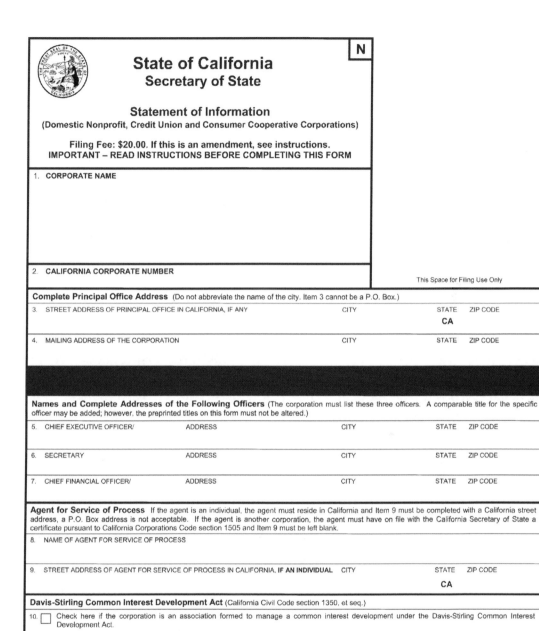

Instructions for Completing Form SI-100

For faster processing, the required statement for most corporations can be filed online at https://businessfilings.sos.ca.gov.

Every domestic nonprofit, credit union and consumer cooperative corporation must file a Statement of Information with the California Secretary of State, within 90 days after the filing of the initial Articles of Incorporation, and biennially thereafter during the applicable filing period. The applicable filing period for a corporation is the calendar month during which the initial Articles of Incorporation were filed and the immediately preceding five calendar months. A corporation is required to file this statement even though it may not be actively engaged in business at the time this statement is due. Changes to information contained in a previously filed statement can be made by filing a new form, completed in its entirety. Credit unions and consumer cooperative corporations are required to file annually instead of biennially.

Legal Authority: Statutory filing provisions are found in California Corporations Code sections 6210, 8210, 9660, or 12570 and California Financial Code section 14101.6, unless otherwise indicated. All subsequent statutory references are to the California Corporations Code, unless otherwise stated. Failure to file this Statement of Information by the due date may result in the assessment of a $50.00 penalty. (Sections 6810, 8810, 9690, or 12670; California Revenue and Taxation Code section 19141.)

Fees: The fee for filing the Statement of Information is $20.00. Checks should be made payable to the Secretary of State. If this statement is being filed to amend any information on a previously filed statement and is being filed outside the applicable filing period, as defined above, no fee is required.

Copies: The Secretary of State will endorse file one copy of the statement if an exact copy is submitted along with the statement to be filed. Copies submitted with the statement to be filed can be certified upon request and payment of $8.00 per copy.

Common Interest Development Association: Every domestic nonprofit corporation formed to manage a common interest development under the Davis-Stirling Common Interest Development Act (for example, a homeowners' association) must also file a Statement By Common Interest Development Association (Form SI-CID) together with the biennial Statement of Information

(California Civil Code section 1350, et seq.). Both forms are available on the Secretary of State's website at www.sos.ca.gov/business/be/statements.htm.

Complete the Statement of Information (Form SI-100) as follows:

Item 1.   Enter the name of the corporation exactly as it is of record with the California Secretary of State.

Item 2.   Enter the corporation number issued by the California Secretary of State.

Item 3.   Enter the complete street address, city and zip code of the corporation's principal office in California, if any. Please do not enter a P.O. Box or abbreviate the name of the city. Note: a credit union must enter the street address of the corporation's principal office, if any, whether the office is located in or outside of California.

Item 4.   Enter the mailing address of the corporation, if different from the street address of the principal office in California or if the corporation has no principal office in California.

Item 5-7. Enter the name and complete business or residential address of the corporation's chief executive officer (i.e., president), secretary and chief financial officer (i.e., treasurer). Please do not abbreviate the name of the city. The corporation must list these three officers. Any number of offices may be held by the same person unless the articles or bylaws provide otherwise, except, in the case of a nonprofit public benefit or religious corporation, neither the secretary nor the chief financial officer or treasurer may serve concurrently as the president or chair of the board (Sections 5213 or 9213). Please note, unless the articles or bylaws provide otherwise, the president, or if there is no president, the chair of the board, is the chief executive officer of the corporation. Additionally, unless otherwise specified in the articles or the bylaws, if there is no chief financial officer, the treasurer is the chief financial officer of the corporation. A comparable title for the specific officer may be added; however, the preprinted titles on this form must not be altered, except in the case of a consumer cooperative corporation, which may include the name and address of its general manager in lieu of the name and address of its chief executive officer. (Section 12570(a).)

Item 8.   Enter the name of the agent for service of process in California. An agent is an individual (director, officer or any other person, whether or not affiliated with the corporation) who resides in California or another corporation designated to accept service of process if the corporation is sued. The agent must agree to accept service of process on behalf of the corporation prior to designation.

If an individual is designated as agent, complete Items 8 and 9. If another corporation is designated as agent, complete Item 8 and proceed to Item 10 or Item 11, as applicable (do not complete Item 9).

Note: Before another corporation may be designated as agent, that corporation must have previously filed with the California Secretary of State, a certificate pursuant to Section 1505. A corporation cannot act as its own agent and no domestic or foreign corporation may file pursuant to Section 1505 unless the corporation is currently authorized to engage in business in California and is in good standing in the records of the California Secretary of State.

Item 9. If an individual is designated as agent for service of process, enter a business or residential street address in California (a P.O. Box address is not acceptable). Please do not enter "in care of" (c/o) or abbreviate the name of the city. If another corporation is designated as agent, leave Item 9 blank and proceed to Item 10 or Item 11, as applicable.

Common Interest Development Corporations: Corporations formed to manage a common interest development under the Davis-Stirling Common Interest Development Act (for example, a homeowners' association) must file a Statement by Common Interest Development Association (Form SI-CID).

Item 10. Check the box only if the corporation is formed to manage a common interest. If the corporation is not formed to manage a common interest development, do not check the box and proceed to Item 11.

Item 11. Type or print the name and title of the person completing this form and enter the date this form was completed.

Completed forms along with the applicable fees can be mailed to Secretary of State, Statement of Information Unit, P.O. Box 944230, Sacramento, CA 94244-2300 or delivered in person (drop off) to the Sacramento office, 1500 11th Street, Sacramento, CA 95814. If you are not completing this form online, please type or legibly print in black or blue ink. This form must not be altered. This form is filed only in the Sacramento office.

ATTACHMENT 4

Collective Expense Allocation Worksheet

Collective Expenses
Monthly (Example 1)

Salaries	6,720
Rent	4,000
Utilities	550
Supplies	500
Misc	200
Legal Reserve Fund	500
Total Monthly Expense	$ 12,470 (a) - Estimate

Expected Visits/Day	30	Multiplied together to get
Average Purchase (grams)	1.5	
Days Open/Month	26	
Estimated Sales	1,170	grams/Mo (b)

(a) Estimated Expense divided by	$ 12,470	
(b) Estimated Sales	1,170	
Expenses per Gram	$ 10.66	(d) - expense allocation per gram (to cover expenses, based on estimates

Cost of Goods Sold (COGS)/Production Cost   Divided by 450

Sky Walker OG	$ 3,500	Per Lb	$ 7.78	per gram	(c1)
Blue Dream	$ 3,200	Per Lb	$ 7.11	per gram	(c2)
Big Bud (Outdoor)	$ 2,200	Per Lb	$ 4.89	per gram	(c3)
Misc (Outdoor)	$ 1,500	Per Lb	$ 3.33	per gram	(c4)

So member price /gram

Sky Walker OG	$ 18.44	(c1) + (d)
Blue Dream	$ 17.77	(c2) + (d)
Big Bud (Outdoor)	$ 15.55	(c3) + (d)
Misc (Outdoor)	$ 13.39	(c4) + (d)

ATTACHMENT 4b

Collective Expense Allocation Worksheet

Collective Expenses
Monthly (Example 2)

Salaries	5,760
Rent	4,000
Utilities	550
Supplies	500
Misc	200
Legal Reserve Fund	500

Total Monthly Expense $ 11,810   (a) - Estimate

Expected Visits/Day	32	Multiplied together to get
Average Purchase (grams)	1.5	
Days Open/Month	26	

Estimated Sales   1,248   grams/Mo (b)

(a) Estimated Expense divided by $ 11,810

(b) Estimated Sales   1,248

Expenses per Gram $ 9.46   (d) - expense allocation per gram
(to cover expenses, based on estimates

Cost of Goods Sold (COGS)/Production Cost   Divided by 450

SFV OG	$ 3,300	Per Lb	$ 7.33	per gram	(c1)
Super Silver Haze	$ 2,800	Per Lb	$ 6.22	per gram	(c3)
Misc (Outdoor)	$ 1,200	Per Lb	$ 2.67	per gram	(c4)

So member price /gram

SFV OG	$ 16.80	(c1) + (d)
Super Silver Haze	$ 15.69	(c3) + (d)
Misc (Outdoor)	$ 12.13	(c4) + (d)

ATTACHMENT 5

Sample Collective Reimbursement
Strain: Sour Diesel
Member: 123 (Mark 1)
Date: 03/15/2012

Note this example assumes :
1. The patient grower cultivated 40 plants on an indoor grow over a three month period and yielded 2 pounds of medicine.
2. * The collective is reimbursing the patient for the grow equipment spread over 6 grow cycles (or roughly two year period). This is by no means required and is an area that the board and member will need to decide on.

Clones	480	40 at $12
Nutrients	250	
Soil/Medium	150	
Electricity	1,500	
Water (allocation)	135	
Rent	1,200	
Grow Equipment* (allocation)	367	$2,200/6 cycles
Travel	110	220 miles at $0.51/mile
Sub Total	$ 4,082	
Labor	110	hours
Rate	$ 25	
Total Labor	$ 2,750	
Total Expense	$ 6,832	(for 2 pounds)
Per lb. price of the Medicine	$ 3,416	

I _____ (patient # 123) declare under penalty of perjury that the information provided on this expense reimbursement spreadsheet is true and correct. I further declare under penalty of perjury that I personally legally cultivated this medicine, I am a medical cannabis patient, a Member of SAMPLE Collective and will not divert any medicine for non-medical use or for use by a non-member. I also acknowledge that I will retain copies of the above receipts (for a period of at least 3 years) as well as a detailed work log. I will provide any requested documents to the Collective within 10 days of notice.

Signed: Date:

ATTACHMENT 6

SAMPLE COLLECTIVE, INC.
MEMBERSHIP AGREEMENT

Sample Collective, Inc., ("Collective") is dedicated to providing our members with high quality health and wellness services pursuant to the Compassionate Use Act and Medical Marijuana Program Act (Health & Safety Code § 11362.5, et seq.). This agreement contains member requirements and guidelines to ensure compliance with the Compassionate Use Act, Medical Marijuana Program Act, the Attorney General Guidelines for the Security and Non-Diversion of Marijuana Grown for Medical Use, (and the City Guidelines); to protect the safety and further the health and wellbeing of members; and to continue to create a member-run, community-based, alternative healing and wellness organization.

I _____, hereby declare and agree as follows:

I reside within _____ County and I am a qualified patient entitled to the protection of California Health and Safety Code § 11362.5, et seq., because my physician has recommended/approved my use of cannabis for medical purposes.

_____ (INITIAL)

My physician has determined that I suffer from a serious medical condition for which medical cannabis provides relief and has provided a written recommendation that verifies this fact. As a condition of membership, I have provided a copy of such recommendation to the Collective, as well as a copy of my current California Drivers License or other recognized form of state issued identification. I understand that the Collective will keep a copy of these documents on file and will independently verify with my physician my medical recommendation that forms the basis of my right to be considered a qualified patient under California law.

_____ (INITIAL)

In order to acquire the medicine my physician recommends, and in accordance with Health and Safety Code § 11362.5, et seq., I hereby seek membership in the Collective and understand that in order to be a member of the Collective, and to maintain my membership in the Collective, I must agree to and follow all terms and conditions set forth in this agreement.

_____ (INITIAL)

I understand that as a member of the Collective, I must contribute finances, labor and/or resources in exchange for membership. Such Contributions are necessary to conduct the day-to-day operations of the Collective for the mutual benefit of its members, which is, but is not limited to, the cultivation and acquisition of medical marijuana.

_____ (INITIAL)

I have been informed and agree that a condition of membership in the Collective requires me to volunteer (hours/ Month or year) in order to contribute to the day-to-day operations of the Collective, provide alternative health and healing services to fellow members of the Collectives, and/or to contribute to the overall wellbeing of the community at large on behalf of the Collective. I have been informed and understand that if I fail to volunteer, my membership in the Collective will be immediately revoked. If I am unable to volunteer as a result of my health and/or physical condition(s), I will provide the Collective a written request for exemption from the volunteer requirement and the Collective shall provide a written response.

_____ (INITIAL)

I have been informed and understand that there will be an annual meeting of all members of the Collective for purposes of voting as to the operation of the Collective and that I will be advised of the annual member meeting by written notice given not less than ten (10) nor more than ninety (90) days before the date of the meeting.

_____ (INITIAL)

I have been informed and understand that the Collective will make available at all times a copy of the Articles of Incorporation, the Bylaws, and any and all amendments to the Bylaws. I also have been informed and understand that the Collective will make available to me upon written request records regarding the reimbursement necessary to compensate patient-members' out-of-pocket expenses, time spent, and any and all expenses incurred in the course of growing and otherwise making available medical cannabis on behalf of the Collective.

_____ (INITIAL)

I agree to be respectful at all times while I am at the dispensary and refrain from disruptive, noisy, inappropriate, violent, or rude behavior. I agree to be respectful of the area adjoining the dispensary and not deposit liter, trash or debris. I agree to refrain from disruptive, noisy, inappropriate, violent, or rude behavior in the areas surrounding the dispensary.

_____ (INITIAL)

I agree not to medicate with cannabis in the areas surrounding the dispensary or on the premises of the dispensary.

_____ (INITIAL)

I understand that the Collective management has the discretion to revoke my membership at any time for any reason, including, but not limited to, non-compliance with any and all conditions of membership set forth in this agreement.

_____ (INITIAL)

I agree to assign agency rights to the Collective for the limited purpose of obtaining legally cultivated medical cannabis and for purposes of growing medication for my benefit. I understand that the Collective is required to possess, transport, and cultivate medical cannabis on my and other members' behalf, and limited authority is granted to the Collective for this purpose.

_____ (INITIAL)

I agree and understand that all medicine obtained is for medical use only and may not be diverted for non-medical use or for use by a non-member of the Collective. I understand that it is a violation of this agreement and of California law to sell or divert my medicine in any way and for any reason to any other person and a violation of this section will result in immediate revocation of my membership in the Collective.

_____ (INITIAL)

I agree to provide the Collective with my current medical recommendation. I understand that any member whose medical recommendation is expired shall be excluded from membership until such time that their qualified status pursuant to the Compassionate Use Act can be verified.

_____ (INITIAL)

I agree that the Collective is the sole and exclusive Collective of which I am a member and, further, that the Collective is the sole and exclusive source of my medical cannabis.

_____ (INITIAL)

I understand that members can possess an amount of cannabis consistent with my medical need. I understand that the Collective may require verification of my medical need by way of a specific physician recommendation or through any means deemed acceptable to the Collective.

_____ (INITIAL)

I understand and agree that my medical cannabis recommendation may be disclosed pursuant to any required audits by any Government agency for purposes of verifying the Collective's compliance with the Compassionate Use Act and the Medical Marijuana Program Act.

_____ (INITIAL)

I _____ declare under penalty of perjury that the information provided on this membership agreement is true and correct. I further declare under penalty of perjury that I am a medical cannabis patient and will not divert my medicine for non-medical use or for use by a non- member. I further declare under penalty of perjury that I am not a member of law enforcement and will not divert any medicine for the purpose of any criminal investigations.

I have read and understand the above requirements and agree to follow these guidelines. Additionally, I hereby authorize the release of my medical information concerning my diagnosis, condition or prognosis to the Collective and its authorized representatives for purposes of verifying the validity of my medical recommendation and the valid operation of the Collective pursuant to the Compassionate Use Act and Medical Marijuana Program Act.

Member Name_____

Member Signature_____ Date_____

ATTACHMENT 7

A Patient's Guide to Recognizing Mold, Mildew and Mites in MMJ
From the Releaf Center

Using The Guide

While an unprecedented number of patients in the state of Colorado now have access to medical marijuana, few have experience with the cultivation and dealing with common pests. A vast majority of cannabis sold in Medical Marijuana Centers has gone through a rigorous inspection process to protect patients from the potential harms that mold, mildew and pests can pose.

This guide is intended to educate patients on ways to identify potential issue without the use of magnifying glasses of expensive microscopes. A well trained eye or nose can spot most damage on the spot.

If you believe you have purchased cannabis that has one of these issues, we suggest that you immediately contact the center from which it was purchased so they can pull any tainted product from their shelves and contact other patients that they may be affected. It can also be helpful to take pictures that identify areas you're concerned with.

The Three M's

Mold:

Botrytis, gray mold, necrotrophic fungus, bud mold...one of the nastiest problems with cannabis goes by many names. Fortunately, it's also one of the easiest to identify.

Mold can cause discoloration

Mold is generally a result of improper humidity levels during the growing or curing stages of processing. Buds with mold present generally lack a strong nose and will remind you more of an old basement than cannabis. Since mold is present where mosisture is trapped, you will need to inspect the center of the bud near the steam. For this reason, larger or dense buds are often more prone.

Mildew:

Powdery mildew (PM) occurs during the cultivation stage and generally attacks the leaves of a plant. It can be difficult to spot as PM appears very similar to trichomes, the wax-like structures on cannabis that give it a "dusted" appearance.

Powdery mildew on cannabis leaves

PM will generally look whiter than a trichome and is fuzzier, as opposed to the elongated structure with tiny heads. It will also be concentrated on the leaves, so make sure to give extra inspection to buds with an extremely tight trim.

Mites:

Spider mites are one of the hardest issues to spot on a finished bud because of their small size. As they feed on plants, discoloration will become evident on the leaves. Dead mites will appear either black or red and small black specks of fecal matter

While spots are often evidence of mite damage

may be present. You may also notice that there will be a crackling or popping noise if you're smoking.

For additional information, please contact The Releaf Center at 303-458-LEAF (5323).

2000 W. 32nd Avenue, Denver CO 80211
http://www.thereleafcenter.com

ATTACHMENT 8

Manual Daily Inventory

Strain	Beginning Inventory	Sales	Grams	1/8ths	1/4s	1oz	Total Sales* (in grams)	Add New Inventory	Expected Ending	Actual Ending^	Variance
Afgooey	222		3	1			6.5		215.5	215.5	0
AK-47	225		6	1			9.5		215.5	215.5	0
Banana Kush	154		2				2		152	147.5	-4.5
Blue Cheese	314		5	2	1		19	227	522	524	2
Blue Dream	315		2			1	30		285	285	0
Bubba Kush	226		2				2		224	224	0
Chemdog	414			1			3.5		410.5	410	-0.5
God's Gift	112		2				2		110	110	0
Grapefruit	343		2				2		341	341	0
Headband	212		3				3		209	207	-2
Hindu Kush	454		3				3		451	455.5	4.5
LA Confidential	321		0				0		321	321	0
Lemon Drop	310		3				3		307	307	0
NYC Diesel	110		0				0		110	110	0
OG	312		5	1			8.5	454	757.5	757	-0.5
Purple Urkle	415		2				2		413	413	0
Romulan	212		3	1			6.5		205.5	205.5	0
Snow Cap	110		2				2		108	108	0
Sour Diesel	212		1				1		211	211	0
Super Silver	316		1				1		315	315	0
Total (grams)	5,309		47	7	1	1	106.5	681	5,883.5	5,882.5	-1

* Note: Use Excel to calculate the total sales in grams. The following equation will calculate all your Standard weights to the metric system /grams (Column D + (column E x 3.5) + column F x 7) + (column G x 28) = total grams sold. Once the work is done setting up the spreadsheet it is easy to use - all that is required is to enter the number of each quantity sold and the program will calculate everything for you. This sheet can be filled out daily or more frequently if needed.

^Per physical count

ATTACHMENT 8A

DAILY SALES
Tally Sheet

Strain	Grams	1/8ths	1/4s	1oz	Notes
Afgooey	III	I			
AK-47	ℍℍ I	I			
Banana Kush	II				
Blue Cheese	ℍℍ	II	I		
Blue Dream	II			I	
Bubba Kush	II				
Chemdog		I			
God's Gift	II				
Grapefruit	II				
Headband	III				

ATTACHMENT 9

Special Notice

STATE BOARD
OF EQUALIZATION

450 N Street
Sacramento
California 95814

BOARD MEMBERS

BETTY T. YEE
First District
San Francisco

BILL LEONARD
Second District
Ontario/Sacramento

MICHELLE STEEL
Third District
Rolling Hills Estates

JUDY CHU
Fourth District
Los Angeles

JOHN CHIANG
State Controller

———————

EXECUTIVE DIRECTOR
RAMON J. HIRSIG

**Board website and
Member contact
Information:**
www.boe.ca.gov

**Taxpayer's Rights
Advocate**
888-324-2798

Information Center
800-400-7115
TDD/TTY: 800-735-2929

June 2007
L-173

Information on Sales Tax and Registration for Medical Marijuana Sellers

1. **What is the Board of Equalization's (BOE) policy regarding sales of medical marijuana?**
   The sale of medical marijuana has always been considered taxable. However, prior to October 2005, the Board did not issue seller's permits to sellers of property that may be considered illegal.

2. **Is this a change of policy?**
   In October 2005, after meeting with taxpayers, businesses, and advocacy groups, the Board directed staff to issue seller's permits regardless of the fact that the property being sold may be illegal, or because the applicant for the permit did not indicate what products it sold. This new policy was effective immediately.

3. **What does the amended BOE policy say?**
   BOE policy regarding the issuance of a seller's permit was amended to provide that a seller's permit shall be issued to anyone requesting a permit to sell tangible personal property, the sale of which would be subject to sales tax if sold at retail. Previously, the Board would not issue a seller's permit when sales consisted only of medical marijuana.

4. **Who is expected to comply with the BOE policy by applying for a seller's permit?**
   Anyone selling tangible personal property in California, the sale of which would be subject to sales tax if sold at retail, is required to hold a seller's permit and report and pay the taxes due on their sales.

5. **Over-the-counter medications are subject to sales tax, but prescribed medications are not. Where does medical marijuana, "recommended" by a physician, fit in?**
   The sale of tangible personal property in California is generally subject to tax unless the sale qualifies for a specific exemption or exclusion. Sales and Use Tax Regulation 1591, *Medicines and Medical Devices,* explains when the sale or use of property meeting the definition of "medicine" qualifies for exemption from tax.

   Generally, for an item's sale or use to qualify for an exemption from tax under Regulation 1591, the item must qualify as a medicine *and* the sale or use of the item must meet specific conditions. Regulation 1591 defines a medicine, in part, as any substance or preparation intended for use by external or internal application to the human body in the diagnosis, cure, mitigation, treatment, or prevention of disease and which is commonly recognized as a substance or preparation intended for that use. A medicine is also defined as any drug or any biologic, when such are approved by the U.S. Food and Drug Administration to diagnose, cure, mitigate, treat, or prevent any disease, illness, or medical condition regardless of ultimate use.

   In order to be exempt, a medicine must qualify under the definition, and it must be either (1) prescribed for treatment by medical professional authorized to prescribe medicines and dispensed by a pharmacy; (2) furnished by a physician to his or her own patients; or (3) furnished by a licensed health facility on a physician's order. (There are some other specific circumstances not addressed here such as being furnished by a state-run medical facility or a pharmaceutical company without charge for medical research.)

STATE BOARD
OF EQUALIZATION
*Special Notice
Information on
Sales Tax and
Registration
for Medical
Marijuana
Sellers*

June 2007
Page 2

Generally, all of these requirements must be fulfilled in accordance with state and federal law.

6. **Many medical marijuana dispensing collectives consider themselves to be health care facilities. Are they exempt from applying for a seller's permit and paying sales tax for this reason?**
Regulation 1591 exempts the sale or use of medicines furnished by qualifying health care facilities. (See response to Question 5, above, regarding the requirements to qualify as an exempt medicine.) State law defines a qualifying "health facility" as either a facility licensed under state law to provide 24-hour inpatient care or a state-licensed clinic.

7. **If I don't make any profit whatsoever from providing medical marijuana, do I still need to apply for a seller's permit?**
Yes. Not making a profit does not relieve a seller of his or her sales tax liability. However, whether or not you make a profit, like other retailers making taxable sales, you can ask your customers to reimburse you for the sales taxes due on your sales, if you fulfill the requirements explained in Regulation 1700, *Reimbursement for Sales Tax.*

As discussed in the response to Question 10, the Board may enter into a payment plan with a seller when the seller has difficulty meeting its tax liabilities. The Board has an Offers in Compromise Program that provides a payment alternative for individuals and businesses who have closed out their accounts.

8. **Is there a way to apply for a seller's permit without divulging the product being sold?**
Yes. The Board will issue a seller's permit to an applicant who does not indicate the products being sold. The applicant, however, will be asked to sign a waiver acknowledging that his or her application is incomplete, which may result in the applicant not being provided with complete information regarding obligations as a holder of a seller's permit, or notified of future requirements by the Board related to the products sold. Applicants who do not wish to indicate the type of products they are selling should leave the line, "What items do you sell?" blank and discuss the issue with a Board representative regarding the incomplete application.

9. **If I have been providing medical marijuana for some time, but have never applied for a seller's permit, will I owe any back taxes?**
Yes. As with any other seller who has operated without a permit, or who has failed to timely file and pay the taxes due, back taxes are owed on any taxable sales made, but not reported and paid. Generally, penalty and interest will also be due.

When you apply for a seller's permit and your application is processed, Board staff will provide sales and use tax returns from prior periods for you to report your sales of medical marijuana and any other products you may have sold, but did not report. You will need to use these returns to self-report all your sales beginning with the month you first started selling taxable products. Once you have filed all your back returns, you will receive a current return for each reporting period in which you make sales. You will continue to receive a return until such time as you stop making sales and have notified the Board of the discontinuance of your business.

The Board, however, may grant relief from penalty charges if it is determined that a person's failure to file a timely return or payment was due to reasonable cause and circumstances beyond the person's control. If a seller wishes to file for such relief, he or she must file a statement with the Board stating, under penalty of perjury, the facts that apply. Sellers may use form BOE-735, *Request for Relief from Penalty,* available on the Board's website.

A seller who cannot pay a liability in full may be eligible for an installment payment agreement. Sellers in need of this type of plan should contact their local Board office, as eligibility is determined on a case-by-case basis.

STATE BOARD
OF EQUALIZATION
*Special Notice
Information on
Sales Tax and
Registration
for Medical
Marijuana
Sellers*

June 2007
Page 3

10. Is there a deadline by which I must apply for a seller's permit?

All California sellers of tangible personal property the sale of which would be subject to tax if sold at retail are required to hold seller's permits. A seller's permit should be obtained prior to making sales of tangible personal property. If you are currently making sales of medical marijuana and you do not hold a seller's permit, you should obtain one as soon as possible. Sellers have a continuing obligation to hold a seller's permit until such time they stop making sales of products that are subject to tax when sold at retail.

11. Where will the money go that is collected from sellers paying this sales tax?

Sales tax provides revenues to the state's General Fund as well as to cities, counties, and other local jurisdictions where the sale was made.

12. Are these tax revenues tied to any specific programs in the state budget?

No. The tax from the sales of medical marijuana is treated the same as the tax received from the sale of all tangible personal property.

13. Does registering for a permit make my sales of medical marijuana any more lawful than they are currently?

Registering for a seller's permit brings sellers into compliance with the Sales and Use Tax Law, but holding a seller's permit does not allow sales that are otherwise unlawful by state or federal law. The Compassionate Use Act of 1996 decriminalized the cultivation and use of marijuana by certain persons on the recommendation of a physician. California's Medical Marijuana Program Act also exempted qualifying patients and primary caregivers from criminal sanctions for certain other activities involving marijuana. Apart from any provisions of state law, the sale of marijuana remains illegal under federal law.

14. Where can I find more information?

Sellers are encouraged to use any of the resources listed below to obtain answers to their questions. They may:

- Call our Information Center at 800-400-7115.
- Request copies of the laws and regulations that apply to their business.
- Write to the Board for advice. Note: For a taxpayer's protection, it is best to get the advice in writing. Taxpayers may be relieved of tax, penalty, and interest charges that are due on a transaction if the Board determines that the person reasonably relied on written advice from the Board regarding the transaction. For this relief to apply, a request for advice must be in writing, identify the taxpayer to whom the advice applies, and fully describe the facts and circumstances of the transaction.
- Attend a basic class on how to report sales and use taxes. A listing of these classes is available on the Board's website at *www.boe.ca.gov/sutax/tpsched.htm*. This page also includes a link to an on-line tutorial for Sales and Use Tax.
- Contact a local Board office and talk to a staff member.

Made in the USA
San Bernardino, CA
06 October 2016